AF332924

GREEK BEAUTY

© 2003 Assouline Publishing for the present edition
601 West 26th Street, 18th floor
New York, NY 10001, USA
Tel.: 212 989-6810   Fax: 212 647-0005
www.assouline.com

First published by Editions Assouline, Paris, France.

Translated from the French by Bernard Wooding.

Color separation: Gravor (Switzerland)
Printed by Grafiche Milani (Italy)

ISBN: 2 84323 551 0

GREEK BEAUTY

BÉRÉNICE GEOFFROY-SCHNEITER

ASSOULINE

To Cassandre, the little nymph, and her grandmother,
who was nicknamed "La Parisienne"…

I served beauty . . .
was it in fact for me
something greater.
(Sappho, 600-500 B.C.)

Penelope, the virtuous and faithful wife; Nausicaa, the young princess; Clytemnestra, the dark monster; Antigone, the rebellious righter of wrongs; Iphigenia, the sacrificed implorer; Athena, the severe virgin; Artemis, the wild huntress; and the most and desirable and beautiful of all, Aphrodite, who forced the gods to submit like mortals to her imperious will. What inner turmoil made your secret souls throb? What fiery passion coursed through even the smallest of your veins? What passionate goad tormented your quivering flesh? Like a dim echo, the poets' verses still resound, and the theories about sculptures and vases, whose mysteries archeologists have rarely succeeded in penetrating, abound, fragile and mute.

"The sacred Heaven feels the desire to penetrate the Earth (Gaia), the Earth is consumed by the desire to enjoy coitus: the rain comes down from the Heaven husband like a kiss toward the Earth, and it gives birth to herds that graze for mortals and the fruit of life of Demeter, as the spring foliage comes to an end under the dew of the hymen, and I am the one who is the cause of all this," proudly

exclaims Aphrodite, the goddess who incarnated burning desire. Away from conventional, academic disquisitions, who will dare to talk about the primordial, cosmic force of love in Greece, the oriental violence of the fragrances and perfumes, the dazzling sight of intertwined bodies, the arching of neck and back? Truncated, perverted, dulled, smoothed, or policed, our vision is based on a multitude of misunderstandings and misinterpretations. The museum pilgrims continue to traipse around, bored with looking at hordes of marble Venuses whose indecent, commonplace curves and countercurves fill mile upon mile of gallery space.

et us make a bold, utopian wish. Let us close our eyes and feel the gentle breeze that wafts toward us from the earliest times—that of a Greece before Greece, the land of the Cyclops, of monsters and sailors. This is a distant and archaic epoch, a time when the goddess Aphrodite was not yet known as Aphrodite, when Homer had yet to sing the first verses of his first songs to the accompaniment of his lyre. Almost five thousand years ago, under the chisels of anonymous masters, strange "marble dolls" emerged, primitive figures whose basic forms have still not yielded their meaning in full. Who are these charming figures, their waists constricted by invisible corsets, faces turned skyward, feet performing a sprightly dance? Are they ancestral goddess mothers? Precious post-mortem concubines? Or, more prosaically, are they simply amulets? Our gaze suddenly alights on the succession of stomachs, whose bulge betrays the unmistakable sign of a fortuitous pregnancy. Sometimes naturalistic, sometimes reduced to a skillful geometric design, often tiny but occasionally almost life-size, these figures that archeologists hastily called "idols" nonetheless represent the first steps of a civilization that was discovering art and the sacred. Indeed, they were originally dotted with ritualistic paint-work and tattoos whose apotropaic value was intended to enhance their primordial function, for it was in the uterine darkness of the grave that these "marble hetaeras" were supposed to reside, near the stone pillows, adornments, and toiletries (pearl necklaces, razors, mirrors, palettes for cosmetics, and bottles of perfumed oils) that had belonged to the deceased. Did the sailors of the Cyclades, like the ancient Egyptians, conceive of death as a voyage, a stepping stone, rather than an ineluctable end? Whatever the answer, these luminous "celestial ballerinas" represent the first sketches of female nudes in their translucent and sepulchral whiteness.

Women truly came of age on another island, located halfway between Greece and Egypt: Crete. "Parisienne" was the racy nickname archeologists bestowed on this charming "coquette's" profile when they first roused it from its millennia-long slumber in the bowels of the palace of Knossos. With her up-turned nose, thick lips, tiny chin, and unnaturally large black eye framed by a mischievous kiss curl, this anonymous Minoan has a youthful, almost profane grace that continues to astonish. Leaving aside the strange red ribbon knotted at the back of her neck and shoulders (also worn by other figures, suggesting some mysterious religious significance), the lovely brunette reflects the fine lifestyle and exquisite refinement of the flourishing kingdom of Crete. With its splendid palaces. women really do seem to have reigned supreme on the island of Minos. With their long skirts brushing against their ankles and black locks dangling down their backs, these gracious priestesses carry out ancient libations to the sound of a seven-stringed lyre or a pair of auloi. Sometimes they appear in pleasant court or banquet scenes as elegant ladies dressed in blue, conversing cheerfully up in their balconies. Such scenes are like snapshots of a civilization in which people lived happily amid a nature both free and tamed, inhabited by monkeys and blue birds, and in which women seem to be the equal of men, or at least their contented companions.

However, there is another, more disturbing side to the mirror. Hieratic and regal, the enigmatic little "Snake Goddess" in the Archeological Museum at Herakleion shoots a death-dealing glance. With her wide-open eyes and brazenly naked breasts, she is in many respects reminiscent of the "mistress of wild animals" of lands further east that were suddenly very close. She also heralds, in her way, the bands of black and chthonic divinities that would soon populate Greek tragedies and the sides of Greek vases. Gorgons with snake-like hair, the Sphinx with the leonine croup, and sirens with bird claws were all bewitching creatures whose hybrid, demonic beauty led to the downfall of many mortals and heroes.

It is perhaps this same expression of "sacred stupor" that one detects in the sepulchral mask dotted with rosettes that conveys, with dread, the clash of weapons from the Mycenean era. Had the exquisite sweetness of the Minoan frescoes, pulsating with happiness and life, faded? Certainly not, for delicate princesses with wavy hair still lived in palaces protected by massive battlements. However, there is no better way of learning about the ideas and beliefs of the Mycenean civilization than to read and reread the work of Homer and the verses written about Hecuba, Andromache, and Penelope.

n o other type of literature shows so clearly the high esteem in which women in Greece were held and the importance attached to the emotion of love there. Even the gods submit to its supreme law! For although Zeus seems to reign with absolute power over a suitably hierarchical Olympus, Hera shows both her strength and her ardent female desire on numerous occasions.

She cleansed all the dirt from her fair body with ambrosia, then she anointed herself with olive oil, ambrosial, very soft, and scented specially for herself—if it were so much as shaken in the bronze-floored house of Jove, the scent pervaded the universe of heaven and earth. With this she anointed her delicate skin, and then she plaited the fair ambrosial locks that flowed in a stream of golden tresses from her immortal head. She put on the wondrous robe which Minerva had worked for her with consummate art, and had embroidered with manifold devices; she fastened it about her bosom with golden clasps, and she girded herself with a girdle that had a hundred tassels: then she fastened her earrings, three brilliant pendants that glistened most beautifully, through the pierced lobes of her ears, and threw a lovely new veil over her head. She bound her sandals on to her feet, and when she had arrayed herself perfectly to her satisfaction, she left her room and called Venus to come aside and speak to her. (Homer, The Iliad, XIV, 170 sq, translated by Samuel Butler)

Is it possible to imagine a more dazzling testament to conjugal love? There then follows a marvelous interlude aimed at proving that Hera's body, beautiful and exquisitely adorned though it is, is still not ready for the amorous encounter. It is lacking that ultimate accessory to seduction: the magic ribbon that Aphrodite, specialist in the arts of the bedroom, wears around her breasts. "As she spoke she loosed from her bosom the curiously embroidered girdle into which all her charms had been wrought—love, desire, and that sweet flattery which steals the judgement even of the most prudent." The passionate wife hides the precious trinket and in a great leap, joins he who has dominion over her heart and senses.

for sure, goddess that she is, the ill-fated Hera spends most of her life experiencing the notorious infidelities of her fickle husband. Indeed, there is an endless list of them, one that tells us rather more about the male fantasies of the Greeks than about the divine nature of Zeus! A whole range of strategies, including abduction, rape, and perfidious tricks of seduction, are used with relish by gods and heroes on vases and in the verses of poems and tragedies. Incarnations of an extreme form of bestial desire, centaurs, sileni, and satyrs, whose hybrid anatomy vividly conveys animal savagery (here a horse's croup, there the horns and hooves of a billy goat), pursue in unambiguous fashion these nymphs and other maenads, who it has been said rarely appear terrified. The same insatiable lust drives Zeus to rape Europa, and impregnate Danae, Semele, and Leda. As we know, Greek art relishes these unnatural couplings, in which the animal combines with the human and monsters are touched by the divine. All is brutal contortion and wild gesticulation, a kind of demonic gymnastics celebrating the cosmic force of the vital principle of "Eros." However, nothing could be less profane than these torrents of orgiastic scenes in which one catches the god Pan in person leaping with insatiable voracity onto a range of victims, from simple shepherdess to proud nymph. Does not this exuberant figure, with his pointed ears, erect phallus, and hairy limbs, celebrate in his own way the regenerative and fertile forces of nature? He is one aspect of what the Greeks saw as the great life force of the universe.

It was inevitable that these creatures, whose very *raison d'être* is a celebration of pleasure and ecstasy, should encounter Dionysus, the god of the grapevine, drunkenness, and desire. As the comic poet Aristophanes aptly put it, "Wine is Aphrodite's milk." The maenads, who were the inseparable companions of the god and his wild, earthy retinue of satyrs with their vigorous phalluses, embody the feminine side of this orgiastic force. The complete antithesis of the well-behaved Athenian woman cloistered away in her apartments, they are outsiders, unbridled savages with panther skins tied around their shoulders and hair flowing in the wind.

> *Oh! lead me, Bromian god,*
> *celestial guide of Bacchic pilgrims,*
> *to the hallowed slopes of Olympus,*
> *where Pierian Muses have their haunt most fair.*
> *There dwell the Graces; there is soft desire;*
> *there thy votaries may hold their revels freely.*
> (Choir, *The Bacchantes*, Euripides, v. 409 ss)

As the illuminating work of Louis Gernet has shown, menaedism is indeed something "exclusively feminine." Not everyone is able to venture into this culture of madness and trance. The Homeric period thus saw the appearance of the disturbing figure of the crazy woman, "stung to frenzied madness" (The Bacchantes, Euripides). Wives taken from their weaving activities, plucked from their homes and their husbands, the maenads accompany Dionysus and his retinue on their ecstatic wanderings. Most strangely of all, they often carry in their arms a new-born baby, which they breastfeed in alternation with young animals such as wolf cubs, peacocks, and snakes. This is a barely disguised allusion to the radically different and wild world of Dionysus, the god of otherness, consumer of raw flesh and disrupter of social categories.

the *korai* (literally, "maidens") unearthed during excavations at the Acropolis in Athens suddenly seem so pleasing and serene to us! These graceful girls, who form a counterpoint to that range of *kouroi* ("youths") whose perfect musculature exalts ardent virility, almost look like coquettes. That, however, would be to overlook their primary function: that being above all, pious ex votos. Apart from the telltale appearance of a mischievous smile (so at odds with the fierce expression of the austere "Auxerre Goddess" in the Louvre), these "marble mannequins" are clad in a cascade of folds that automatically bring to mind, many centuries later, the beautiful dresses and tunics of Mariano Fortuny! Should we see this marble effervescence as evidence that Greece of Ionia was fond of make-up and perfumes? A long way from the stiffness of the Dorian *peplos* (the very one worn by the fierce Athena on that famous stele), these abundant folds reveal more than they conceal the delightful shapes of these young creatures. The *himation* (a woolen cloak) is generally fastened at the right shoulder and passes diagonally across the chest, forming, on either side of the body, cascades of divergent folds. The *chiton,* a thin tunic of pleated linen generally fastened at the right shoulder, clings tightly to the breast that is not covered by the cloak, while revealing the shape of the back and the tapering of the legs (although the arrangement of the garb has its own rather eccentric architecture, the Ionian artist was more concerned about the decorative effect created than about plain reality). Onto this symphony of clothing is grafted the choreography of the headdress, made up of subtle variations of curls and coils, undulations and twists, in which one can just detect, here and there, the line of a tiara or the sparkle of an ear pendant. Let us give thanks for the caprices of history that have made possible the conservation, miraculously intact, of these notes of color that restore the freshness of an embroidery or the velvety softness of a look. The eye wanders tenderly across this spruce assembly of young girls, proud in their beautiful garments. Archeologists have with relish given them pretty nicknames, such as "The Coquette" or "The Sulky One."

a s Jean Charbonneaux, specialist in Greek sculpture, aptly puts it: "The day the *kouroi* and the *korai* stopped smiling, classical art was born." The fifth century began with an unprecedented political crisis that led Athens from tyranny to democracy, from the Ionic style to the "severe" style. Naturalism, sobriety, and impassivity were the new watchwords. Gone were the feminine curves indulgently modeled by the chisels of voluptuous sculptors! The facile seductiveness and other such affectations became a thing of the past. From now on, the folds of the *himation* had to fall straight, in parallel with the long, neat braids of their hair. The gentle *korai* were forced to swap their lovely grace for a reserved expression of pious reflectiveness. Jean Charbonneaux went as far as to compare their perfectly oval faces to those of the most chaste of Florentine madonnas.

t his was not a time for the glorification of the female body. Virile, glorious, heroic, and anthropocentric, that was how the fifth century saw itself. Or rather, that was the aspect it wanted to present to the world through its effigies carved in marble or cast in bronze. It was as if man had succeeded in defeating his demons and monsters and gained mastery of the world through his own strength. Indeed, the century of Pericles was marked by these admirable conquests in democracy, history, and tragedy. It was a century when heroes were transformed into statues in the very heart of the agora (in the middle of the main square in Athens, and the tyrannicides of Critius and Nesiotes celebrated the fall of tyranny and the birth of a new regime), a century of artistic ferment (the city was a vast construction site that drew artists and craftsmen from all over Greece), and a century of social change, as well. At a time when portraiture was appearing for the first time (the affirmation of a new dimension now known as individualism), the artist also dared proclaim the stamp of his genius. There was Phidias, of course, who was responsible for the megolomaniac construction project of the Parthenon, not to mention Alcamenes, Agoracritus, and Polycletus, as well as those painters ("drawers" would be a more appropriate word) who transcribed on the sides of vases the founding myths of the city.

A veritable icon of this period of self-celebration, the "Doryphorus," or "Spear Bearer" (alas known only through the Roman marble copy, a pale reflection of the original, in the Museo Archeologico Nazionale, Naples), serves as a sort of artistic manifesto. Its perfect proportions (the overall height is seven times that of the head) obey the strictest of canons. It is based on a subtle balance spread between the limbs, the load-bearing leg corresponding to the relaxed arm, the relaxed leg to the active arm, while the bend in the hip is counterbalanced by the shoulder sloping in the opposite direction. Many sculptures would adopt ad nauseam this arithmetical system based on measure and balance: muscular figures of Heracles, young athletes with the headband of victory tied around their foreheads, and even Aphrodites with sober, unfeminine anatomies.

and yet, as the fifth century was drawing to a close, a time when the Greek world was ravaged by war and its dominant values were beginning to crumble, the goddess of love made something of a comeback. This can be seen in the emergence of sculptures that glorify the brilliance and radiance of her beauty, in a nudity that was increasingly bold. These include: the "Esquiline Aphrodite," a torso in the Louvre which displays a sensuality that is hardly in keeping with restrained classicism (the breasts are relatively small, but the delicate modeling of the lower abdomen and the way her polished thighs rub against each other are surprising for such an early period); the "Aphrodite with Pillar," whose relaxed body in supple repose provides a pretext for a breathtaking display of folds that highlight the ample forms of the model; and the "Venus Genetrix," whose right arm is depicted in a flirtatious gesture, while the left hand holds out a pomegranate, the symbol of fertility.

However, it was not until the beginning of the fourth century that the first full-fledged nude appeared under the sensitive chisel of Praxiteles. Although the "Aphrodite of Arles," one of the master's youthful works, represented a timid and partial unveiling (only the goddess's bust emerges from a cascade of folds, an approach adopted several centuries later by the anonymous author of the "Venus de Milo"), the "Aphrodite of Cnidus" glows in her sacred fullness. Down the centuries, few sculptures have provoked such devotion, or even wild passion as well.

One can only admire on a modest level, the string of copies or adaptations that emerged in the wake of this supreme nude. And yet there is nothing profane, and certainly nothing vulgar, in this marble beauty surprised in the act of bathing. By devoting herself to her ritual ablutions, the goddess of love and desire is simply regenerating the extraordinary and sacred charisma that inhabits every part of her body. This applies to the position of her right hand, which could perhaps be concealing what the modesty of simple mortals requires that one hide. Alternatively, in a gesture that is forcibly significant given that it is being made by the most beautiful of Olympian women, it could on the contrary be indicating the sexual organ as a fertile source of pleasure and life. Playing wonderfully on the ambiguous, the art of Praxiteles could thus be seen as harking back long centuries to the ancestral attitude of the most ancient of goddess mothers.

Sacred fervor does not exclude sensuality, however. Thus legend has it that it was the perfect body of the courtesan Phryne, the sculptor's own companion, that served as the model for this supreme nude. The inspired chisel of the talented Nicias (it is important to imagine this delicate marble "warmed up" by the pale pigments diluted in the wax applied by his esteemed collaborator) thus gave birth to a masterpiece of religious piety as well as a troubling testament to amorous passion. Praxiteles' followers were in no doubt, some placing greater emphasis on the flesh, others on the composition. From the goddess surprised while bathing, Aphrodite gradually became a "coquette" crouching to let the waves wash over the sensual curves of her anatomy. Suddenly we are a long way from the *thambos,* or "divine astonishment," that overcame pilgrims when seeing this incarnation of desire in all its fatal necessity.

Soon, the Hellenistic period would become crazy about these amorous images, which eventually provided a pretext for nudes that were increasingly oriental and well endowed. Endlessly depicted on mirror covers and on the sides of vases, Aphrodite was almost reduced to the level of home decoration! Aphrodite gazing at herself in the mirror, Aphrodite adjusting her hair, Aphrodite undoing a sandal, Aphrodite doing up the band that serves as a bra, the poor goddess is spared nothing, not even the smallest dimple in the back, or even the slightest bulge in the throat leading to an exaggeration of sometimes dubious taste.

It is questionable as to whether or not the "Venus de Milo" should be consigned to this gallery of alluring, or perhaps even old-fashioned nudes? The great Romantic German poet Heinrich Heine described her as "Our Lady of Beauty." She was by turn revered, decried, and parodied. What extraordinary mystery has led this spiral of white marble to fascinate sculptors and painters and hold those modern-day pilgrims of art (museum-goers) spellbound?

Certainly, such renown demands a harsh ransom: exhumed in the nineteenth century, the "Venus de Milo" (in fact it would be more accurate to call this Greek sculpture the "Aphrodite of Melos") has attained the ambiguous status of an icon: perfect, remote, inviolable, untouchable, but admittedly also "archetypal" or even "commonplace." Has studying the goddess so intently led to a dulling of desire? If only we could have forgotten how to look at that majestic and imperious face haloed with exquisite gravity, that "splendid stomach, as broad as the sea" (to borrow the inspired words of Auguste Rodin), the admirable twist in that turning bust, and the small of the back that is unlike any other. The identity of the inspired master who glorified this flesh is not important. He may have been a neoclassical sculptor, an artist from that Greece of Asia Minor so expert in affairs of love. It is tantalizing to think that the creator of the "Venus de Milo" lived in the same cultural and geographical climate (even if centuries and miles separated them) as that other eulogist of the games of Aphrodite and Eros: Sappho.

much rambling prose has been written about the passionate feelings between the poetess of Lesbos and her students and young companions. The expressions "Sapphic love" and "lesbian passion" have passed into everyday usage and are still applied to those relationships that the Greeks no more regarded as reprehensible in the case of men than in the case of women. This is clear when you look at, submerged in the sea of images of courtesans or female slaves being made love to by men, those few bas-reliefs showing reposing Bacchantes, whose conjoined bodies are comparable to the voluptuous physical couplings of the odalisques in the *Turkish Bath*.

This passionate lover confided to a certain Agallis: "Whenever I catch sight of you, even if for a moment, / then my voice deserts me / and my tongue is struck silent, a delicate fire / suddenly races underneath my skin, / my eyes see nothing, my ears whistle like / the whirling of a top / and sweat pours down me and a trembling creeps over / my whole body, I am greener than grass, / at such times, I seem to be no more than / a step away from death" (translated by Josephine Balmer).

a n admirable interpreter of her own amorous turmoil (in her verses she rages against "love the looser of limbs"), Sappho has nevertheless become the indirect spokesperson for all those women of ancient Greece that poets and tragedians inevitably looked at through male eyes. The poet's pen gave birth to a genuine women's love literature in the noblest sense of the term, encompassing troubled confessions of jealousy, the bitchiness and fiery arguments that occurred among this little circle of friends and musicians, the fondness for perfumes and ointments, and the passion for beautiful clothes and bodies. She is neither dull nor conventional. She is very immodest and very modern, as testified by these few verses describing, with poignant lucidity, the approach of old age and with it, the vanishing of beauty:

Age seizes my skin and turns my hair
From black to white:
My knees no longer bear me
And I am unable to dance again
Like a fawn.
What could I do? I am not ageless:

My youth is gone.
Red-robed Dawn, immortal goddess,
Carried Tithonus to earth's end
Yet age seized him
Despite the gift from his immortal lover...
I love delicate softness:
For me, love has brought the brightness
And the beauty of the sun...
(*Oxyrhynchi Papyri*, 1787,
fragment 58, translated by D. W. Myatt)

to defeat the scars of passing time and combat the treacherous wrinkle and the sagging flesh, magic potions and miraculous ointments were invented. We know, through numerous allusions, that courtesans (unquestionably the most emancipated people in the city!) were not the only women to use artificial aids to seduce men. In his comedy *Lysistrata*, Aristophanes mentions all the means used by respectable Athenian women to arouse desire in their husbands, or their lovers: "These are the very armaments of the rescue. / These crocus-gowns, this outlay of the best myrrh, / Slippers, cosmetics dusting beauty, and robes / With rippling creases of light." Were not these the best strategies for a wife to distract her bellicose husband's attentions from war?

Elsewhere, a fragment by a comic poet reveals how women of little virtue passed on their beauty secrets from one generation to the next: "Once they have begun earning money, they take an interest in the young women who are starting out in the profession. They reshape them and change their external appearance. This one is too small? We put cork in her shoes. This one is too tall? She must wear thin slippers and walk with her head resting on her shoulder, which makes her smaller. And this one has no hips? She wears a bustle and the spectators go wild about her beautiful behind. Like the actors, they have false breasts. They arrange them so they are erect and hold their dresses out in front of them like poles. Their eyelashes are too thin? They dye them with lamp black. They are too dark? They coat them with ceruse. If the courtesan's skin is too white, she applies make-up. If part of her body is pleasing, she exposes it. She has beautiful teeth? She tries to laugh all the time so that those present can admire the mouth she is so proud of. If she does not feel like laughing . . . she keeps a fine branch of myrtle between her lips, so that she has to smile whether she wants to or not. (Fragment 18, Alexis).

but woe betide those whose recalcitrant husbands abhor tricks and ploys! Ischomachus in Xenophon's *The Economist* recounts: "I one day noticed she was much enameled with white lead, no doubt to enhance the natural whiteness of her skin; she had rouged herself with alkanet profusely, doubtless to give more colour to her cheeks than truth would warrant; she was wearing high-heeled shoes, in order to seem taller than she was by nature." (Translated by H. G. Dakyns.) The austere moralist attempts to show the ill-fated flirt the superiority of natural beauty over artificial beauty created by means of make-up. However, such sermons were to little or no avail, judging by the popularity of perfumes and other cosmetics in ancient Greece, and much later in distant al-Fayyum, not to mention Rome and Pompeii.

But if there is one accessory that sums up all the ambiguous traps of seduction, the destructive and ephemeral dangers of beauty, it is the mirror and the blurred reflection in its bronze disk. Reproduced endlessly on the sides of vases and on funerary stelae, its mere outline, next to that of a distaff, suffices to conjure up a specifically female environment.

i n the most inspired poems of the Greek Anthology (a collection of short texts dating from the seventh century B.C. to the tenth century A.D.), it is synonymous with passing time, the symbol of the unbearable fading of beauty. Under the name of Plato (although the attribution is contested by philologists), one can read: "I whose haughty laugh taunted all Greece, I who had a swarm of young people in my antechamber, I dedicate my mirror to the goddess Paphos, for I do not want to see myself as I am, and I cannot see myself as I used to be." However, one thing is clear, like the delicate sandals, false curls, gilt belts, precious ribbons, transparent bras, and boxwood combs, the mirror is an exclusively female item. Men who have them are of "suspect" sexuality, like the bodyguards of Helen in Euripides' *Orestes,* escorts of servants "in charge of mirrors and perfumes," which some claim could have been eunuchs from Asia. In his *Thesmophoriazusae,* Aristophanes, for his part, portrays the poet Agathon as a "man-woman." The mirror, as one would expect, reveals the female side of this ambivalent character, together with those other tricks of seduction such as small bottles, hairnets, dazzling dress, and bra.

And yet nothing could be more perverse than the intimate relationship between the mirror and beauty: first, because beauty is always ambivalent, and second, because seduction often causes infinite suffering. Like Pandora, the beautiful Helen alone embodies the weight of this curse. Yet Aphrodite, in her treacherous cruelty, has only accorded mortals an ephemeral beauty, a fleeting image that has vanished as soon as it is reflected in the mirror. She alone enjoys the privilege of being able to gaze at her reflection and admire herself without displeasure. Recounting the preparations of the famous beauty competition presided over by Paris, Callimachus utters the following explicit phrase: "Cypris [another name for Aphrodite], several times, holding the shining bronze, redid the curls in her hair." The Hellenistic poet compared the flirtatious goddess to her two rivals: "Neither Hera nor Athena looked at their features in the bronze disk, nor in the diaphanous waters of the Simois." We know the outcome of the mythical competition, which ended in the brilliant victory of Aphrodite and for Paris, the love of that most beautiful of mortals—"Helen of a thousand mirrors destined to enjoy a deadly fame. Here, 'beauty' is synonymous with 'fate'."

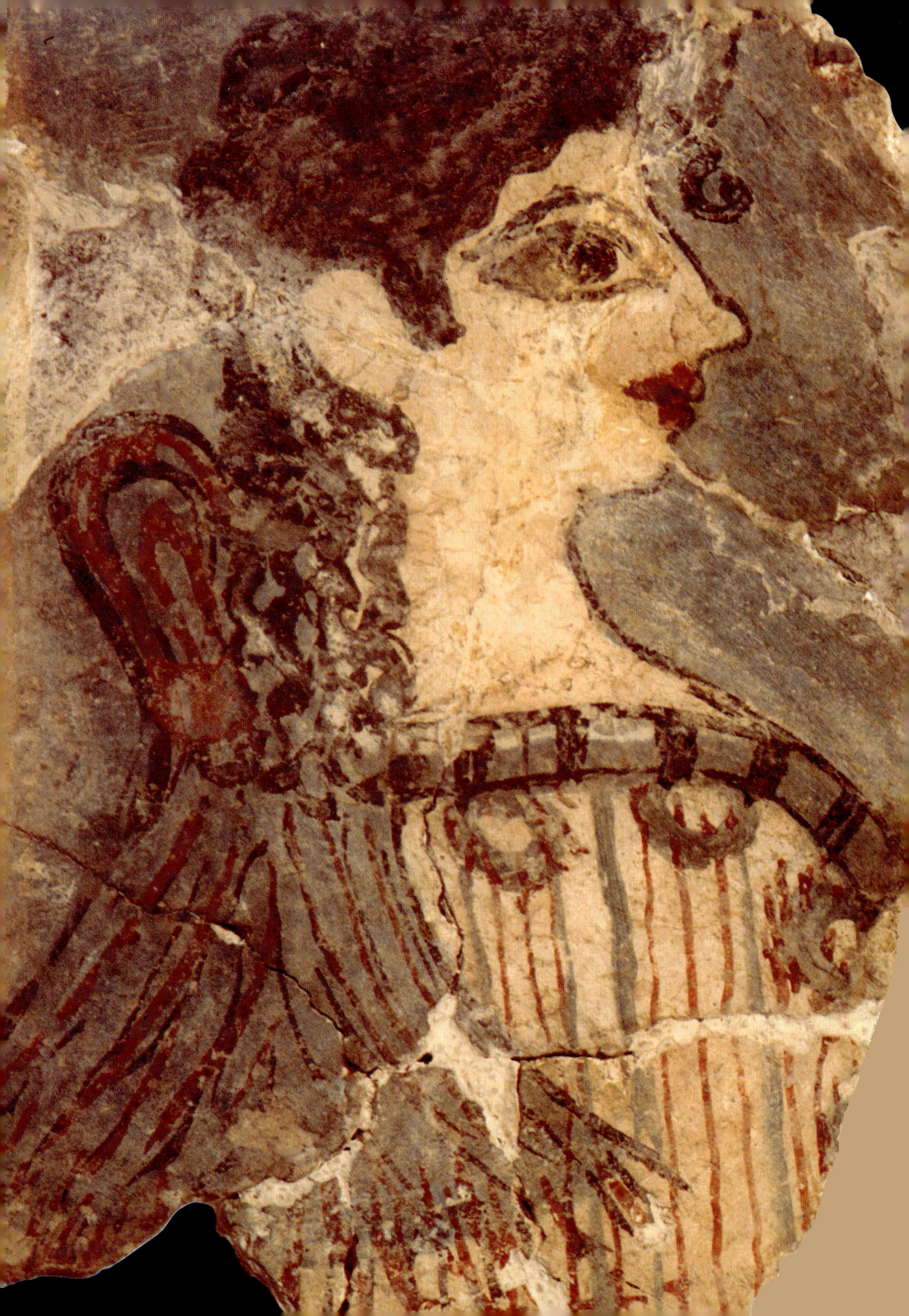

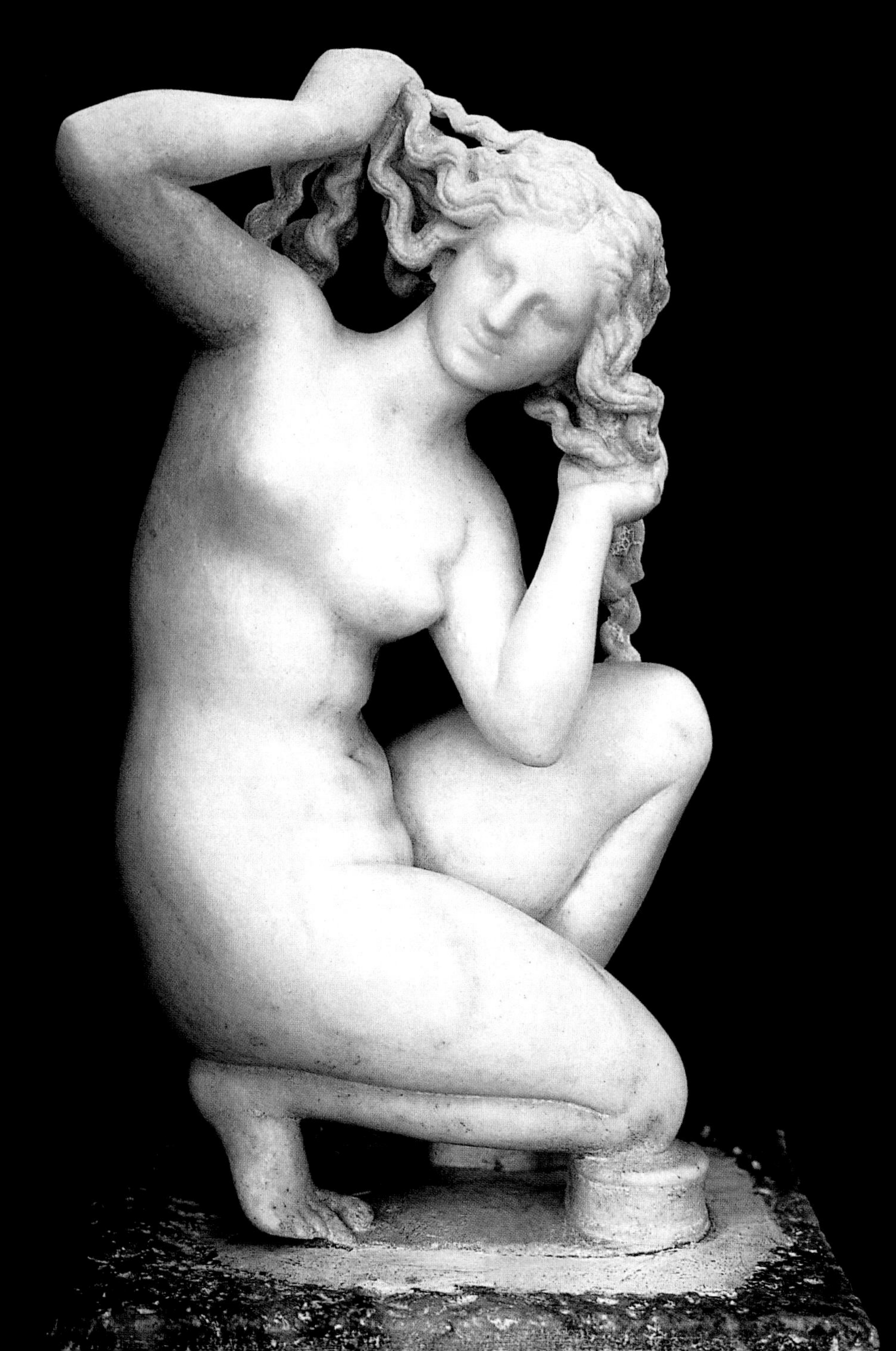

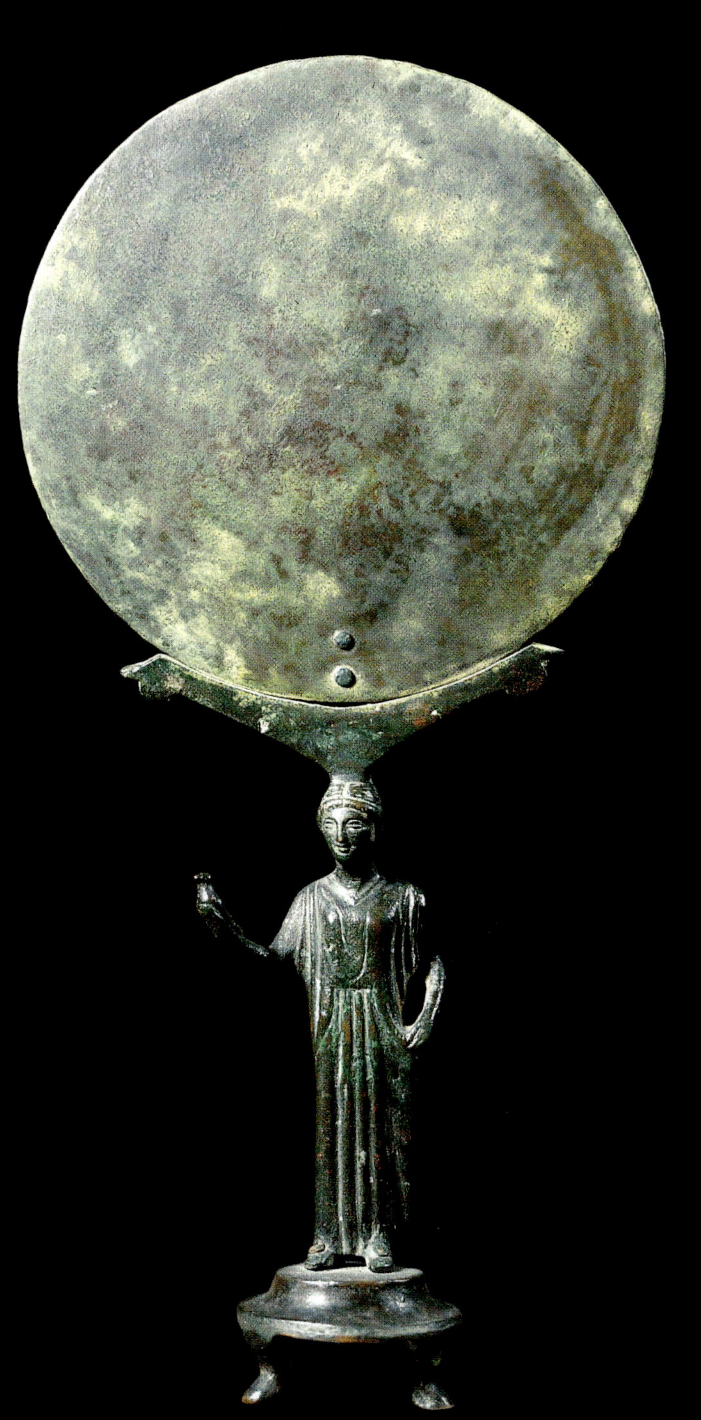

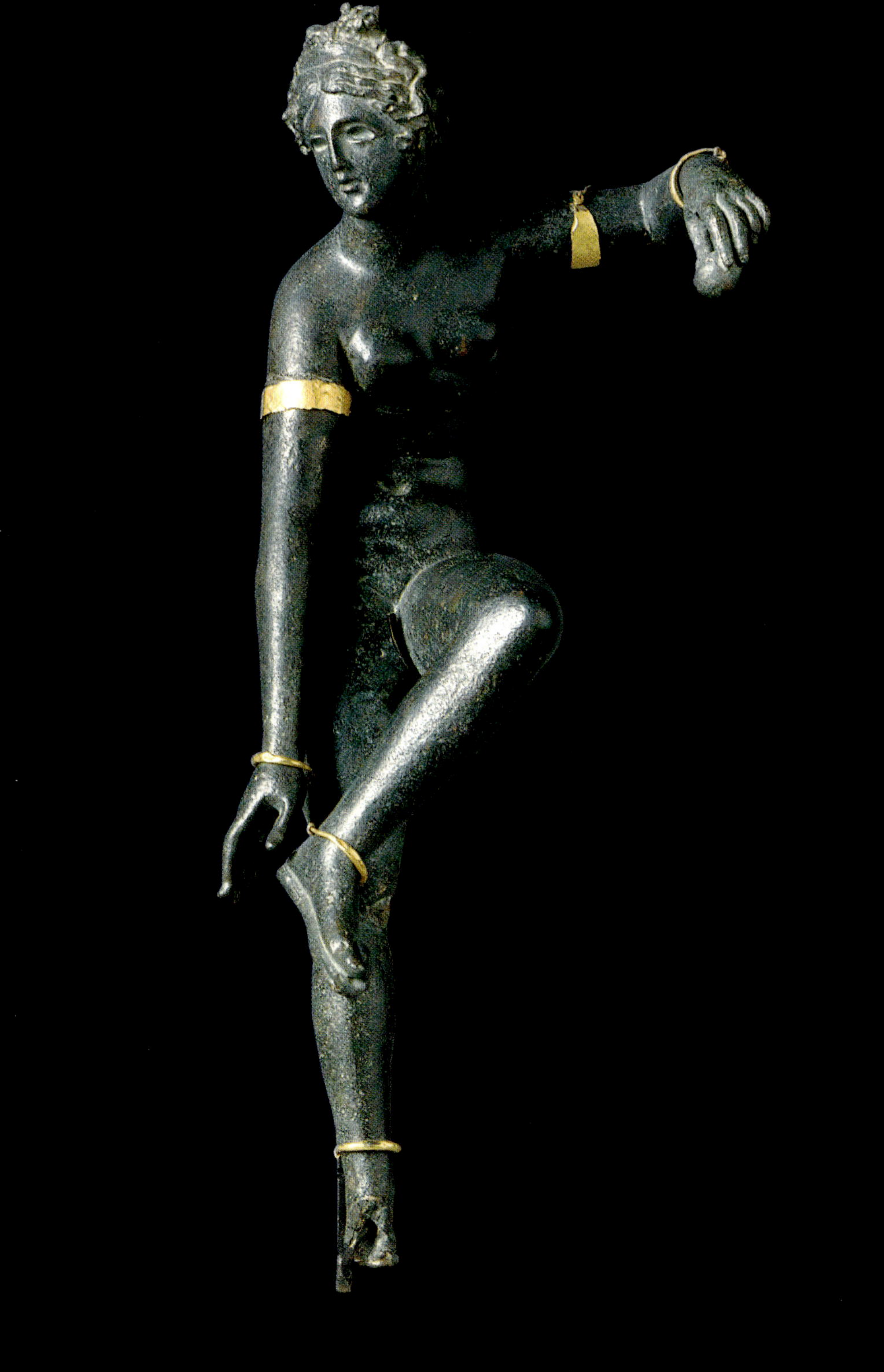

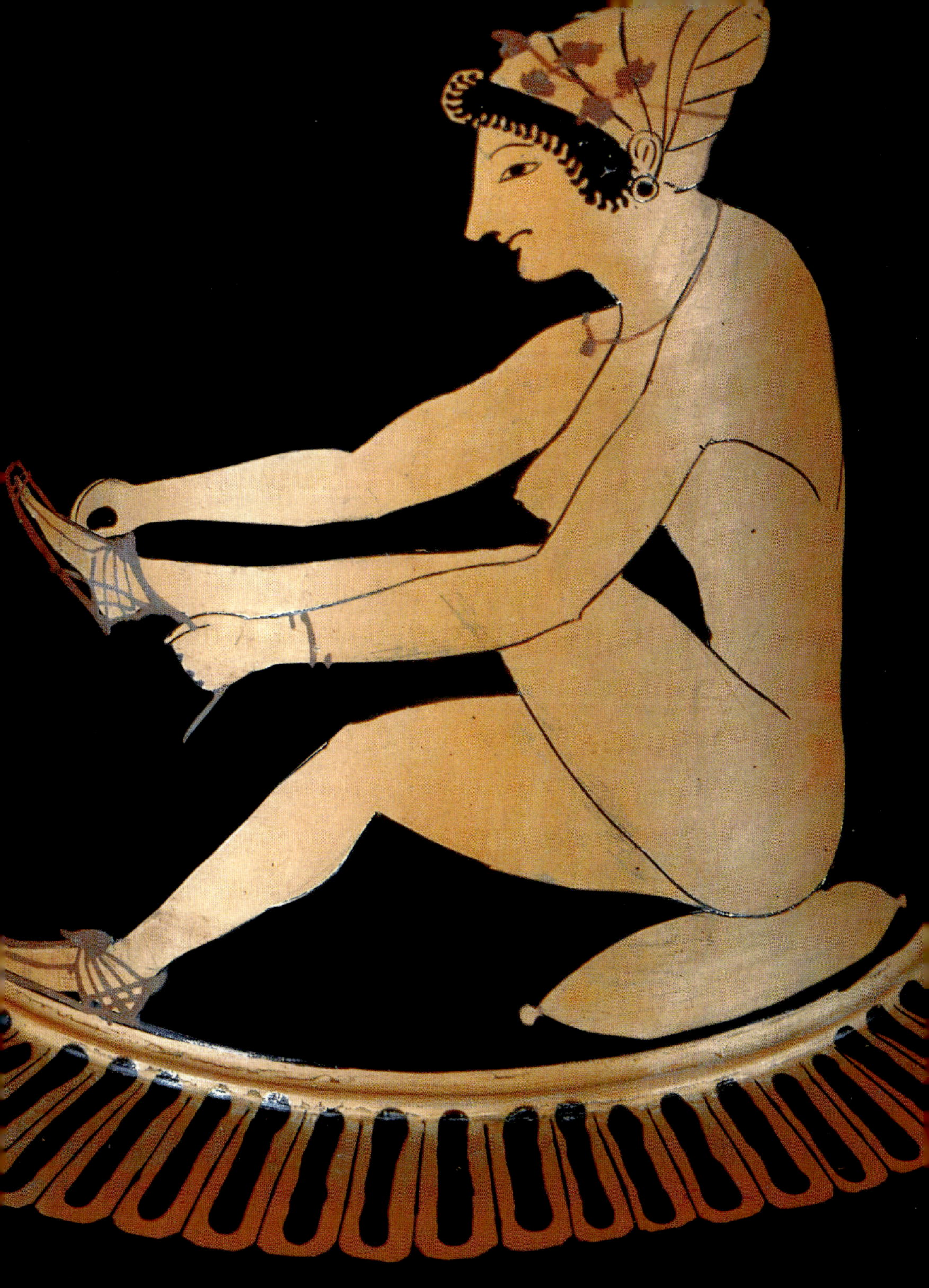

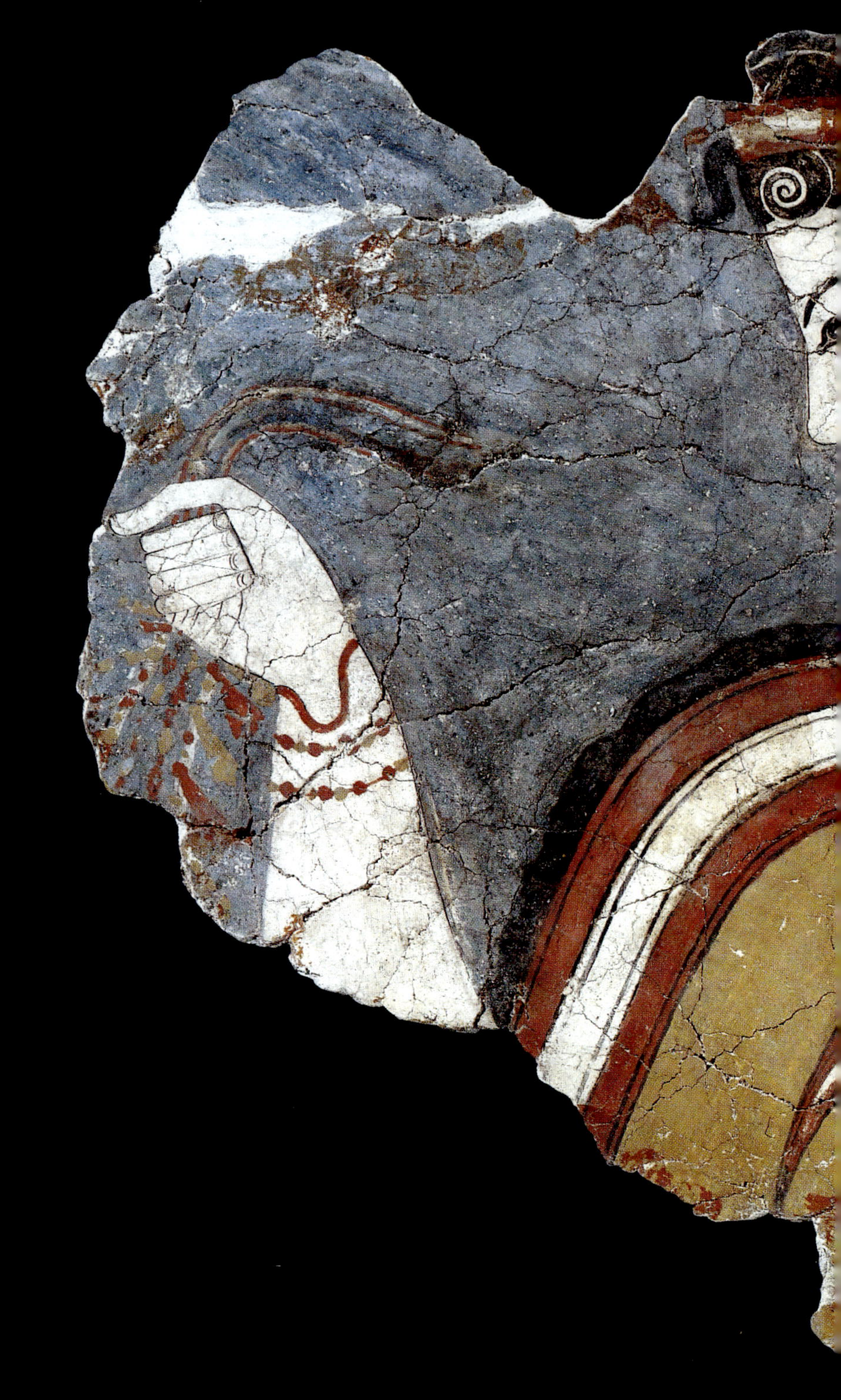

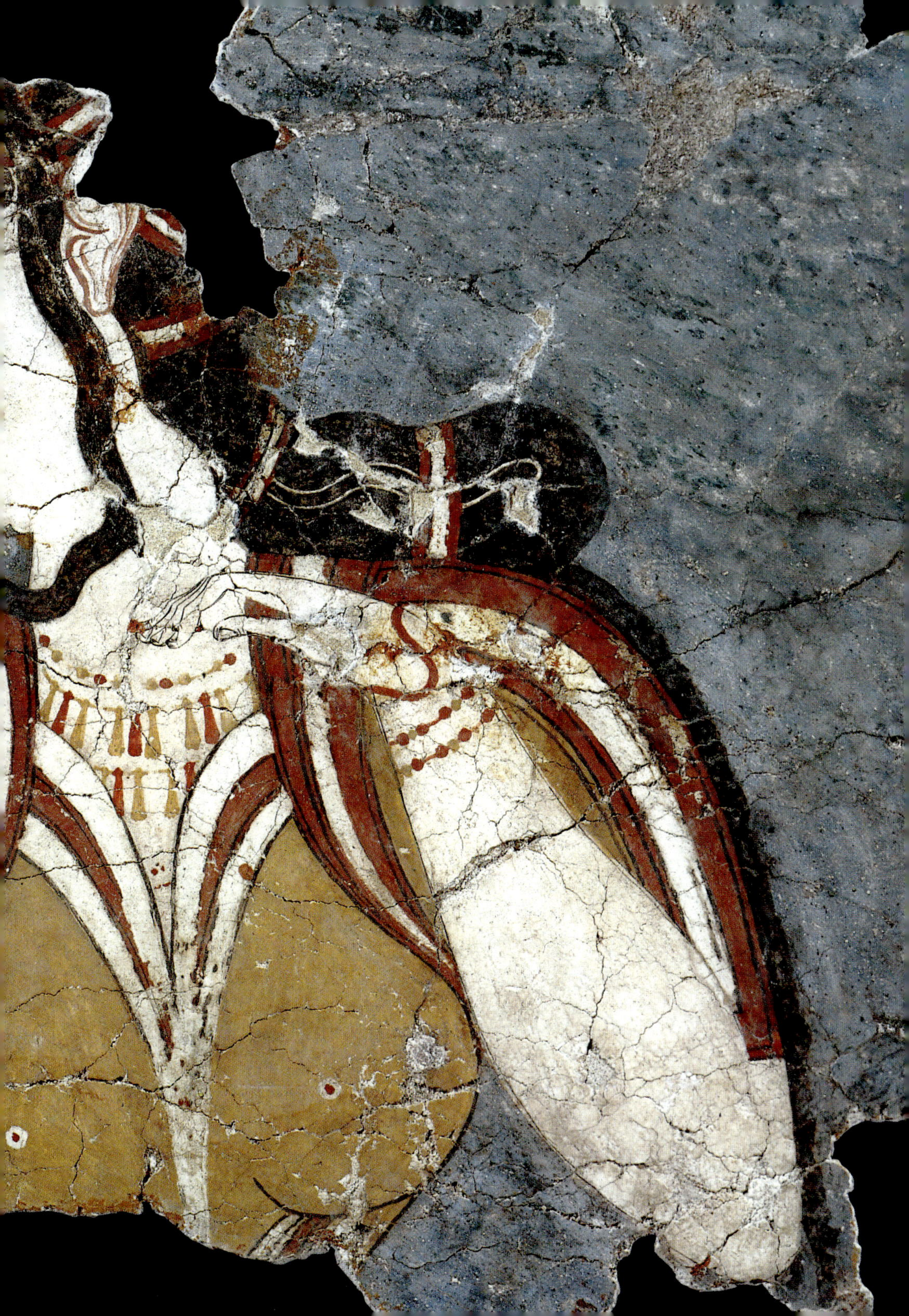

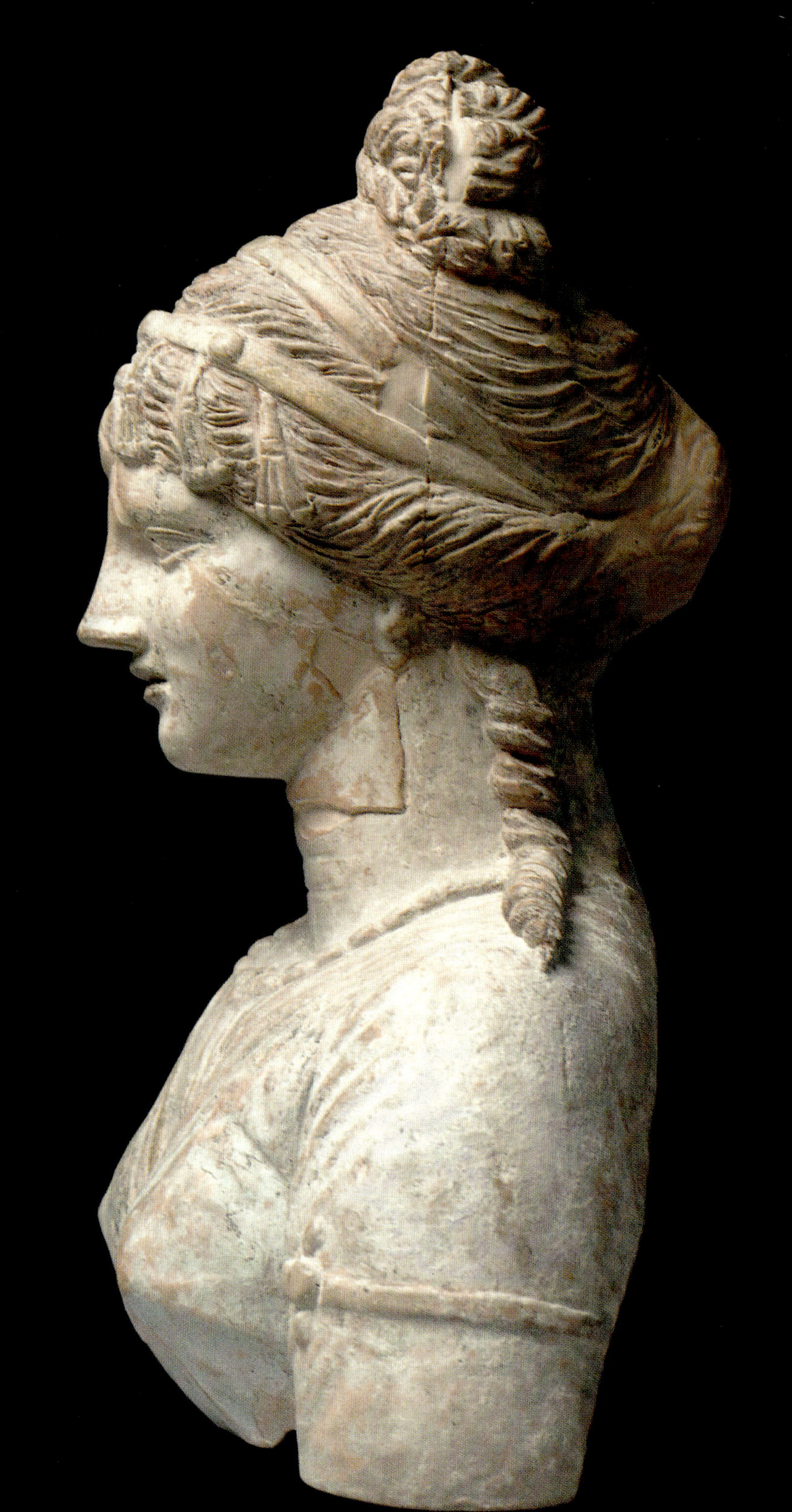

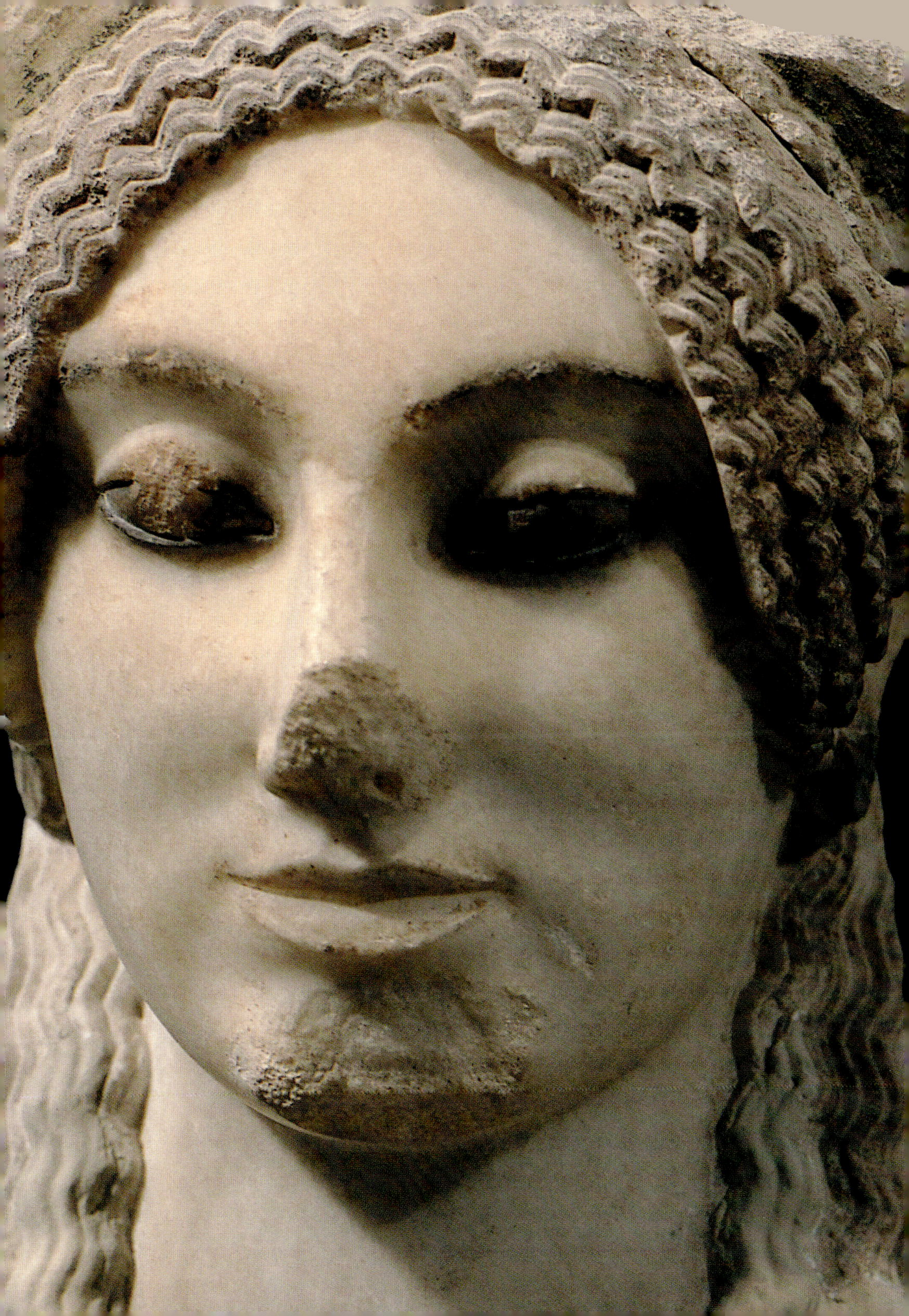

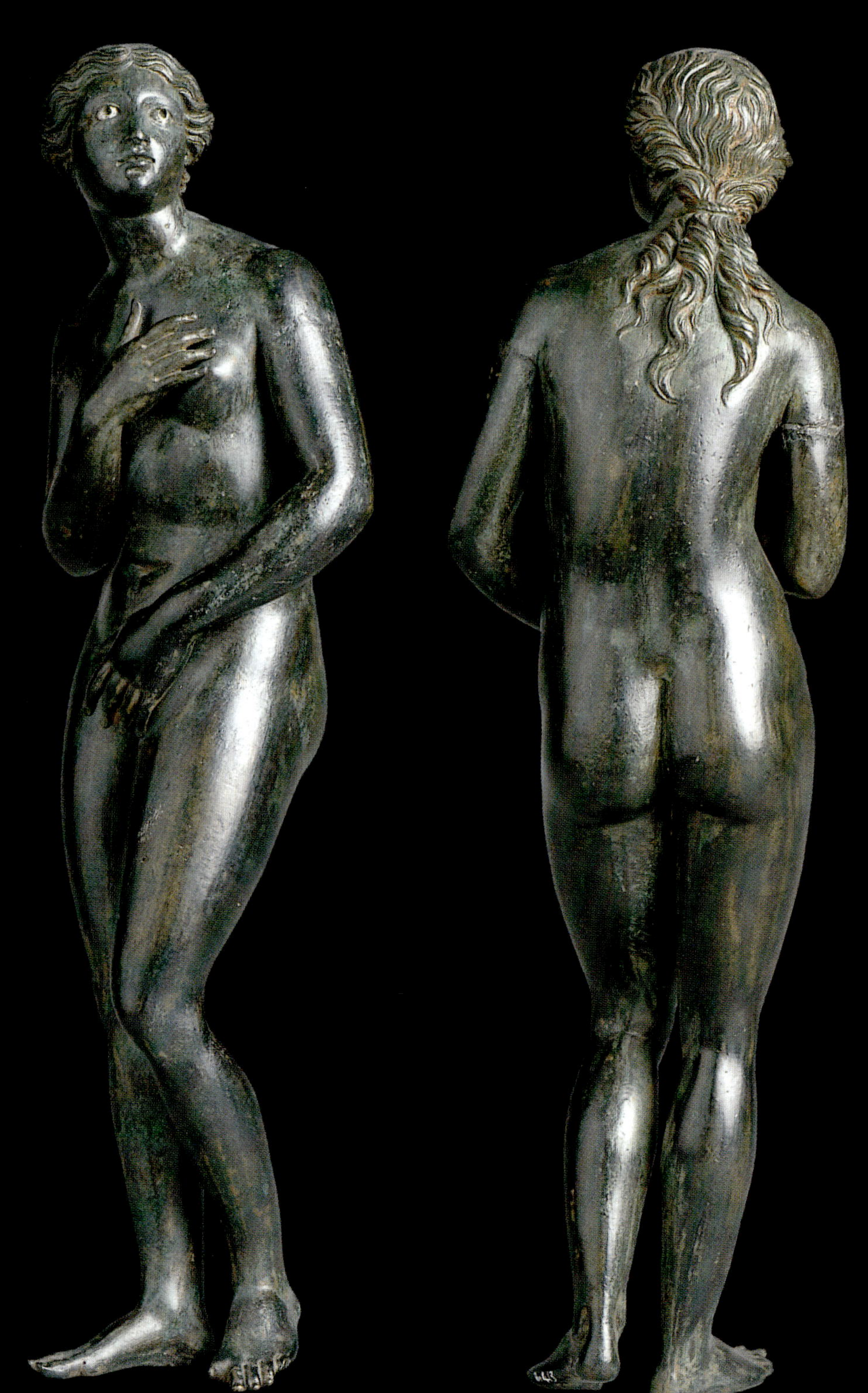

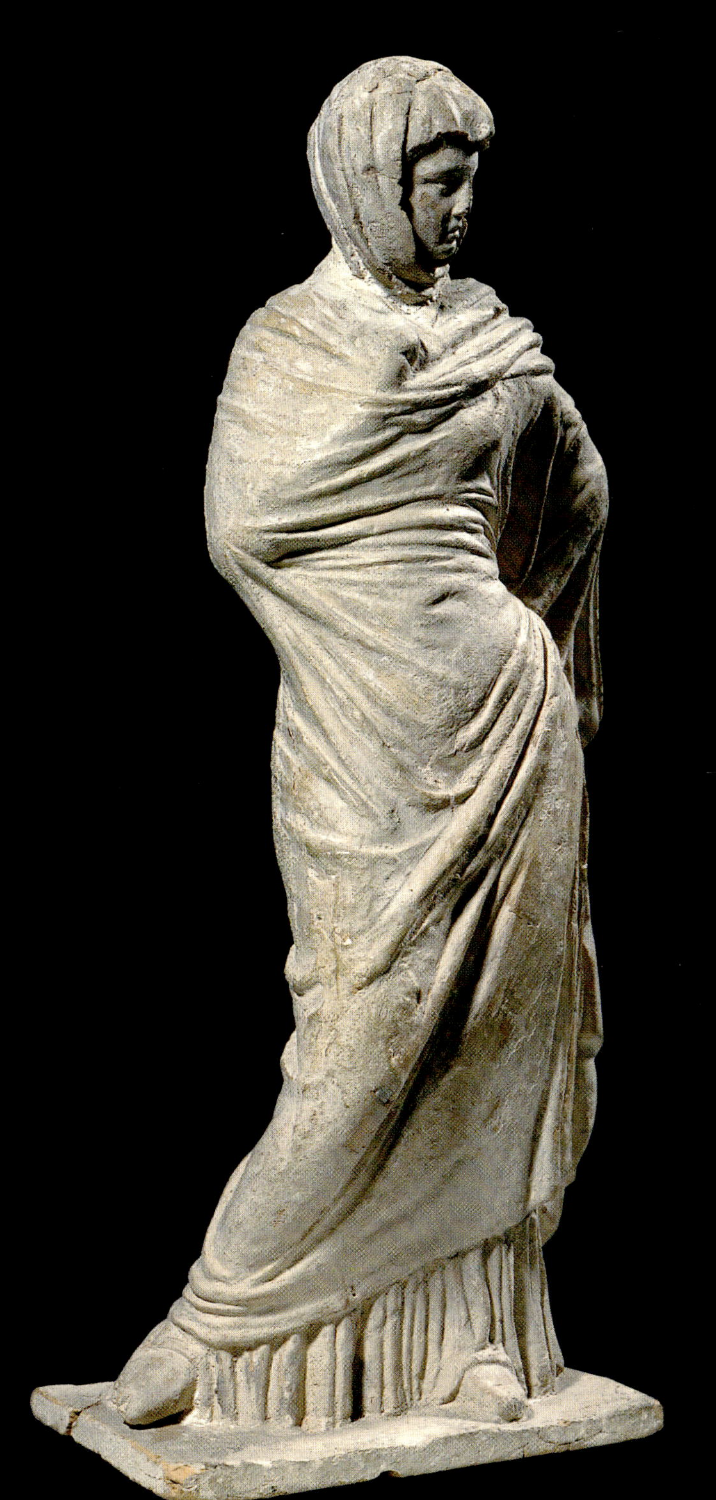

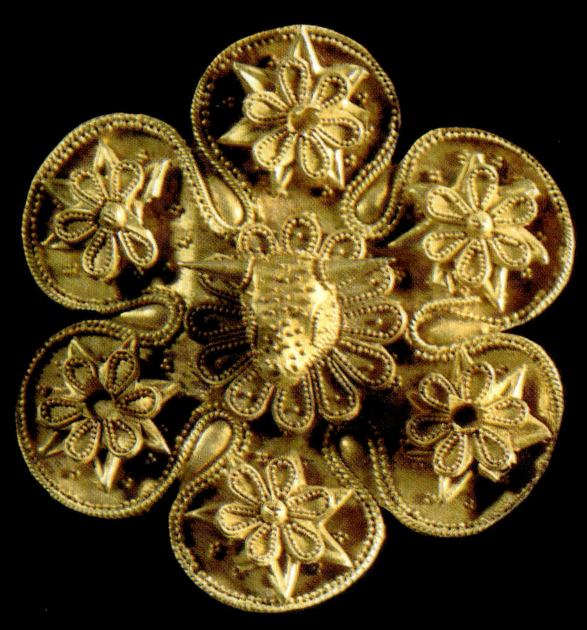

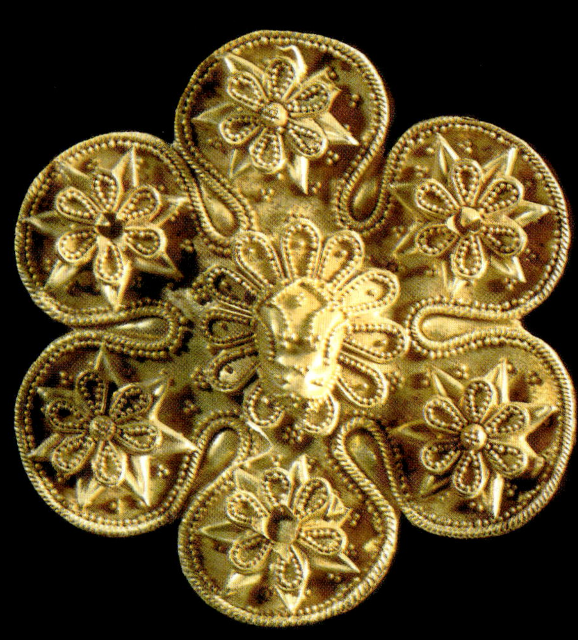

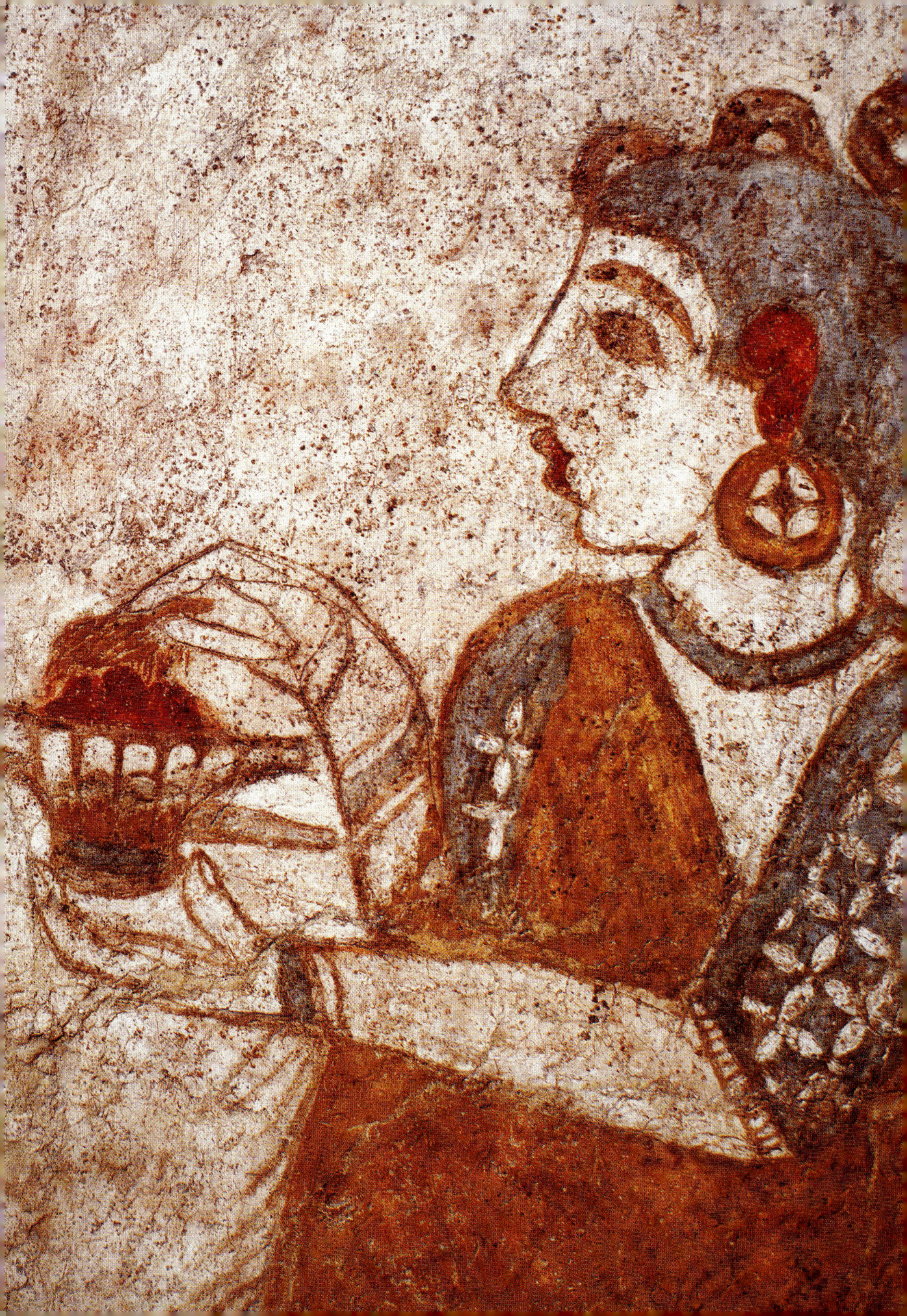

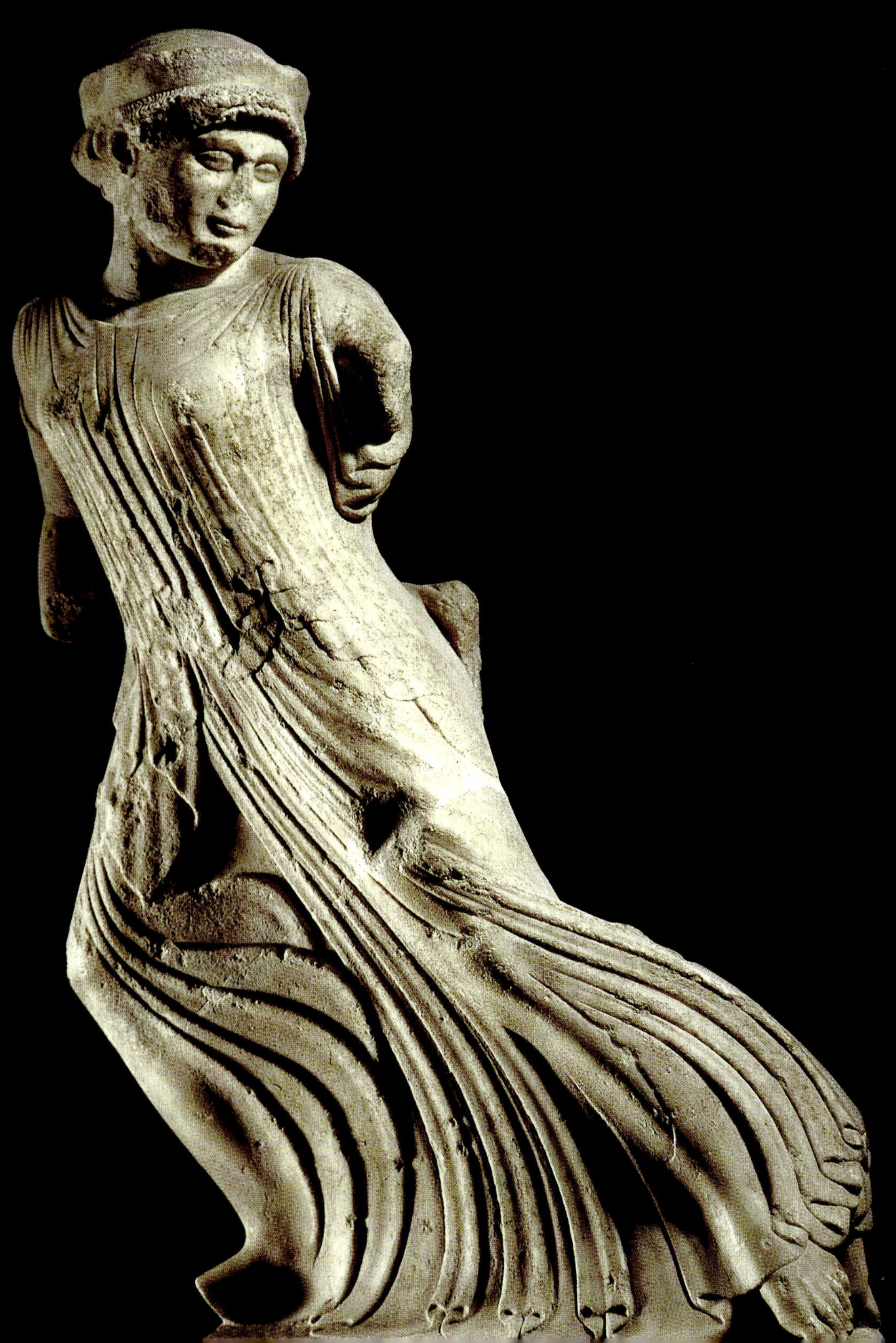

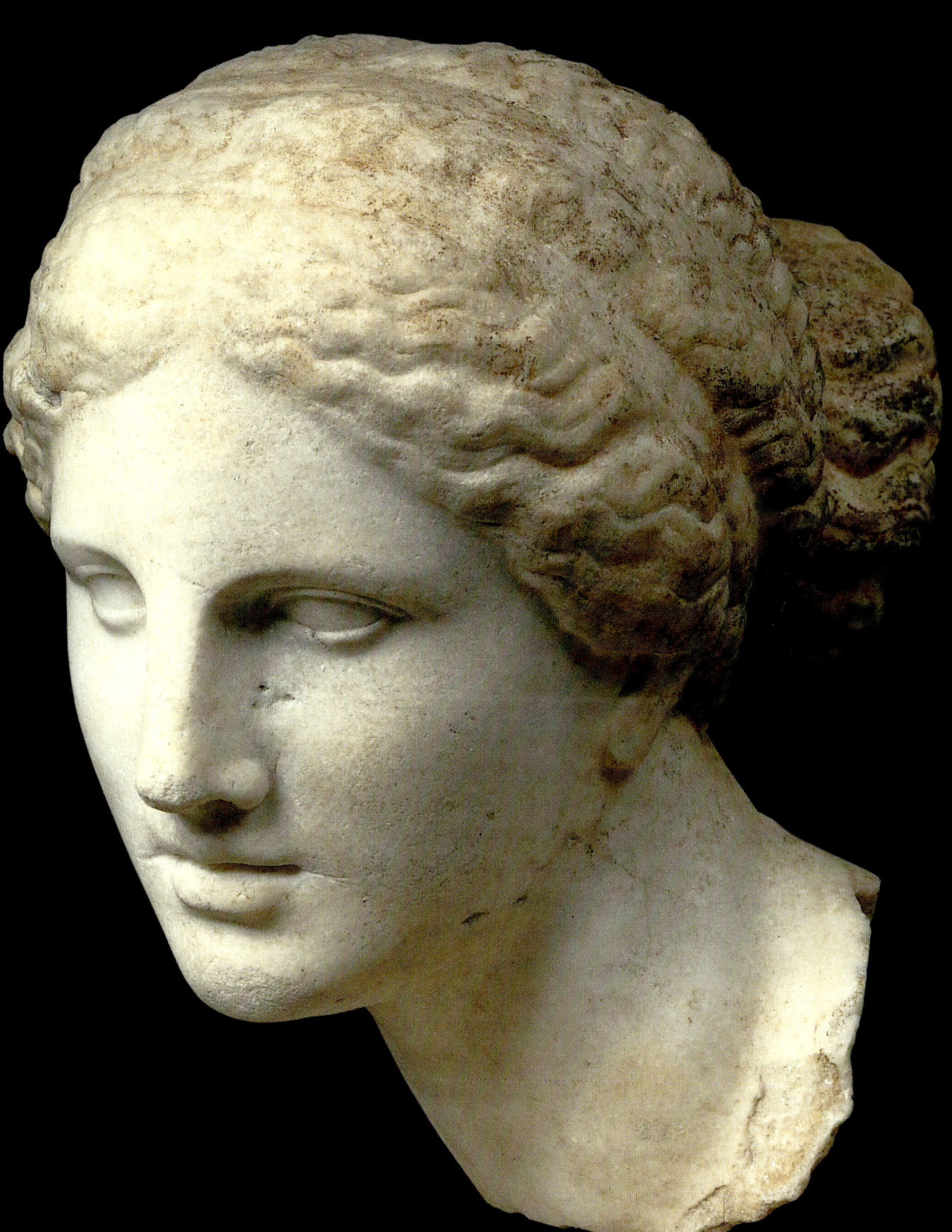

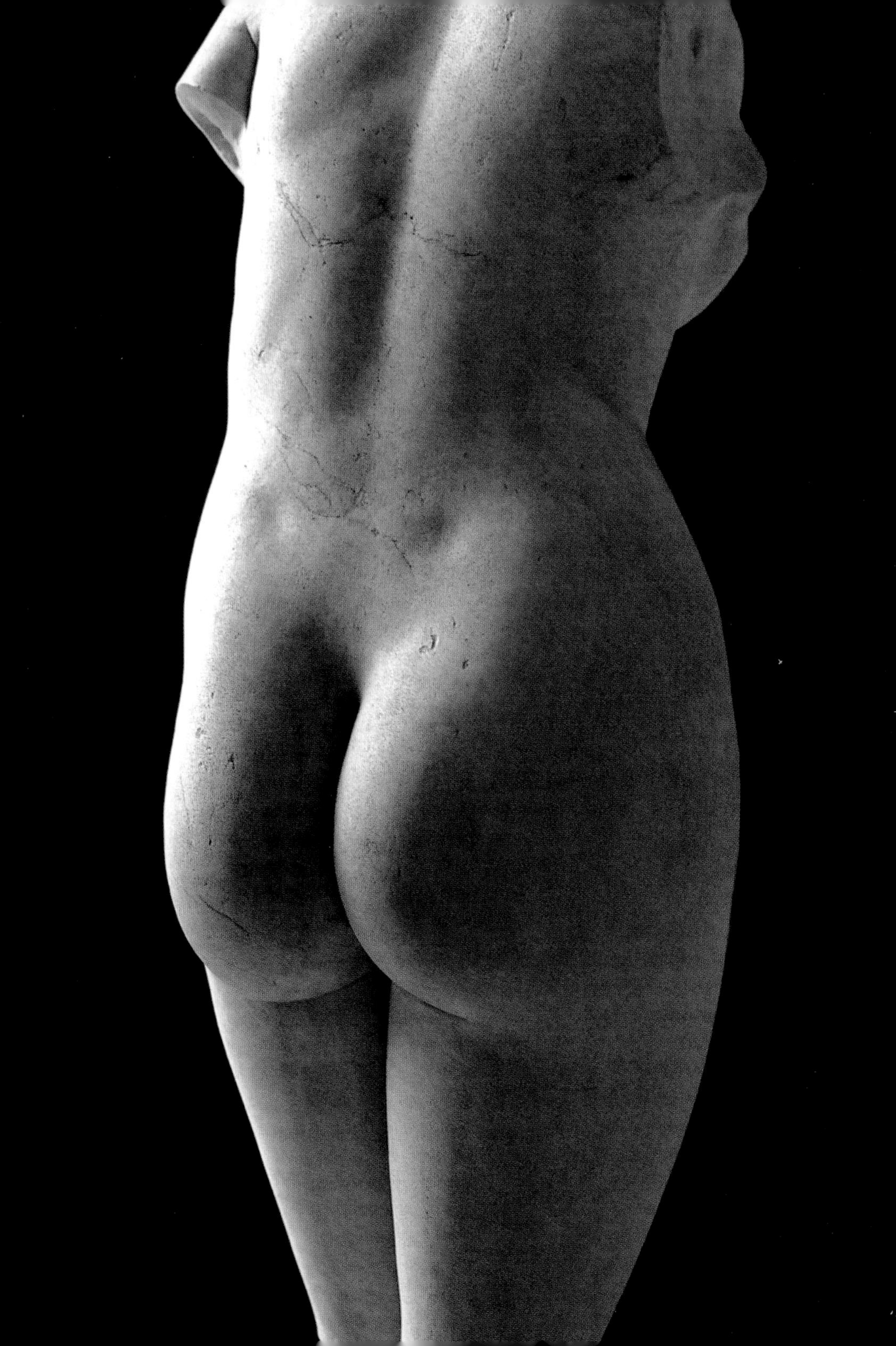

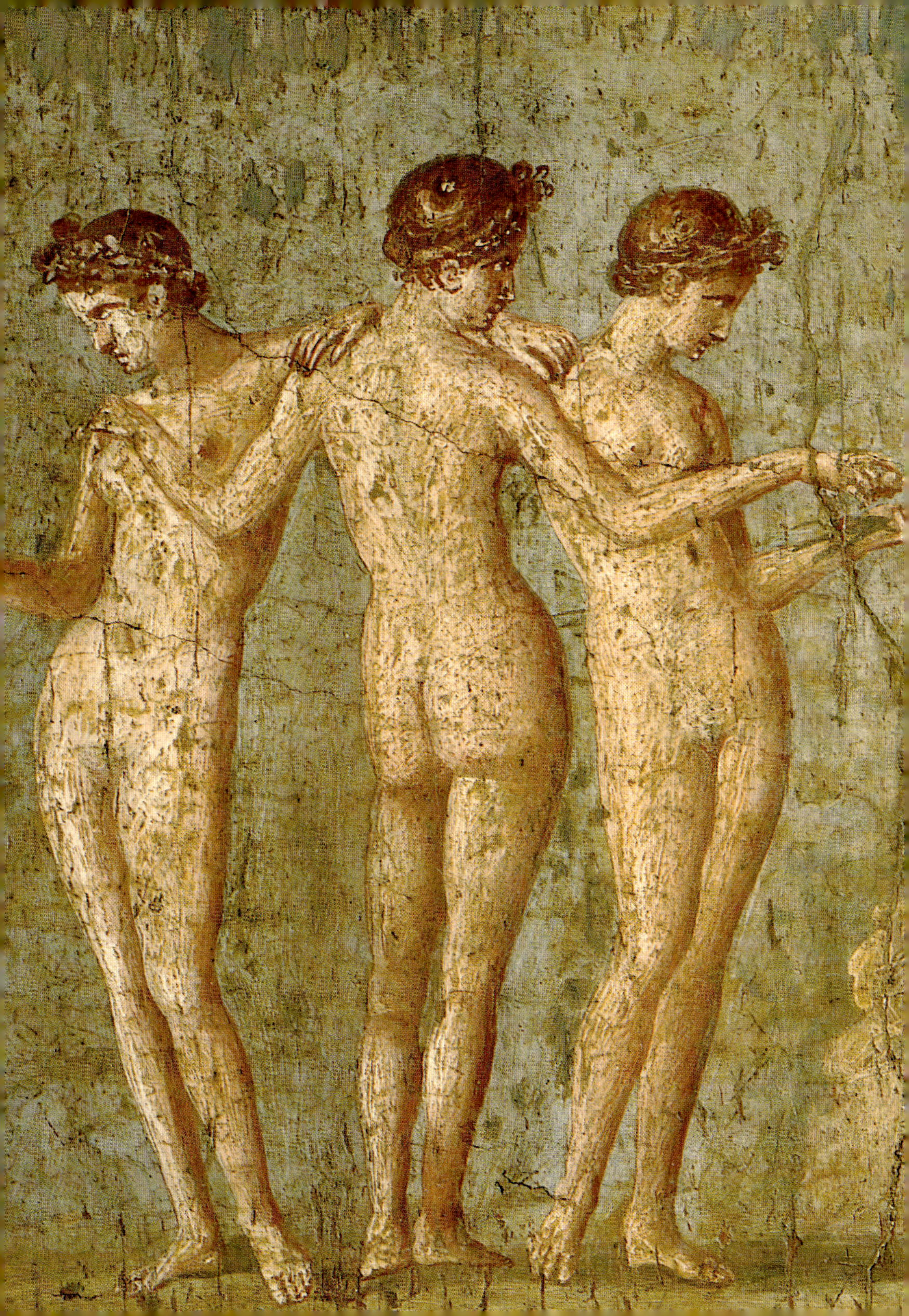

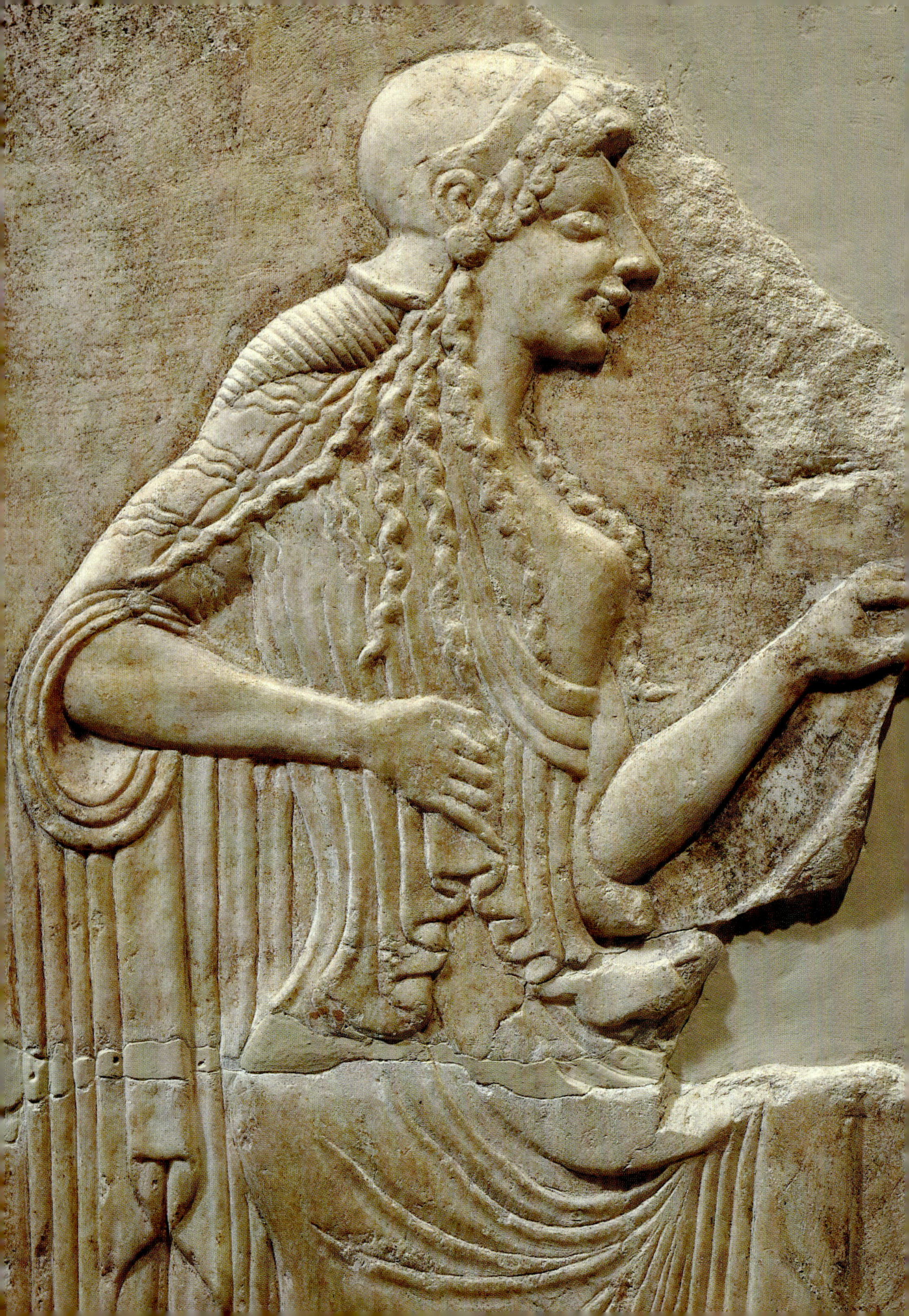

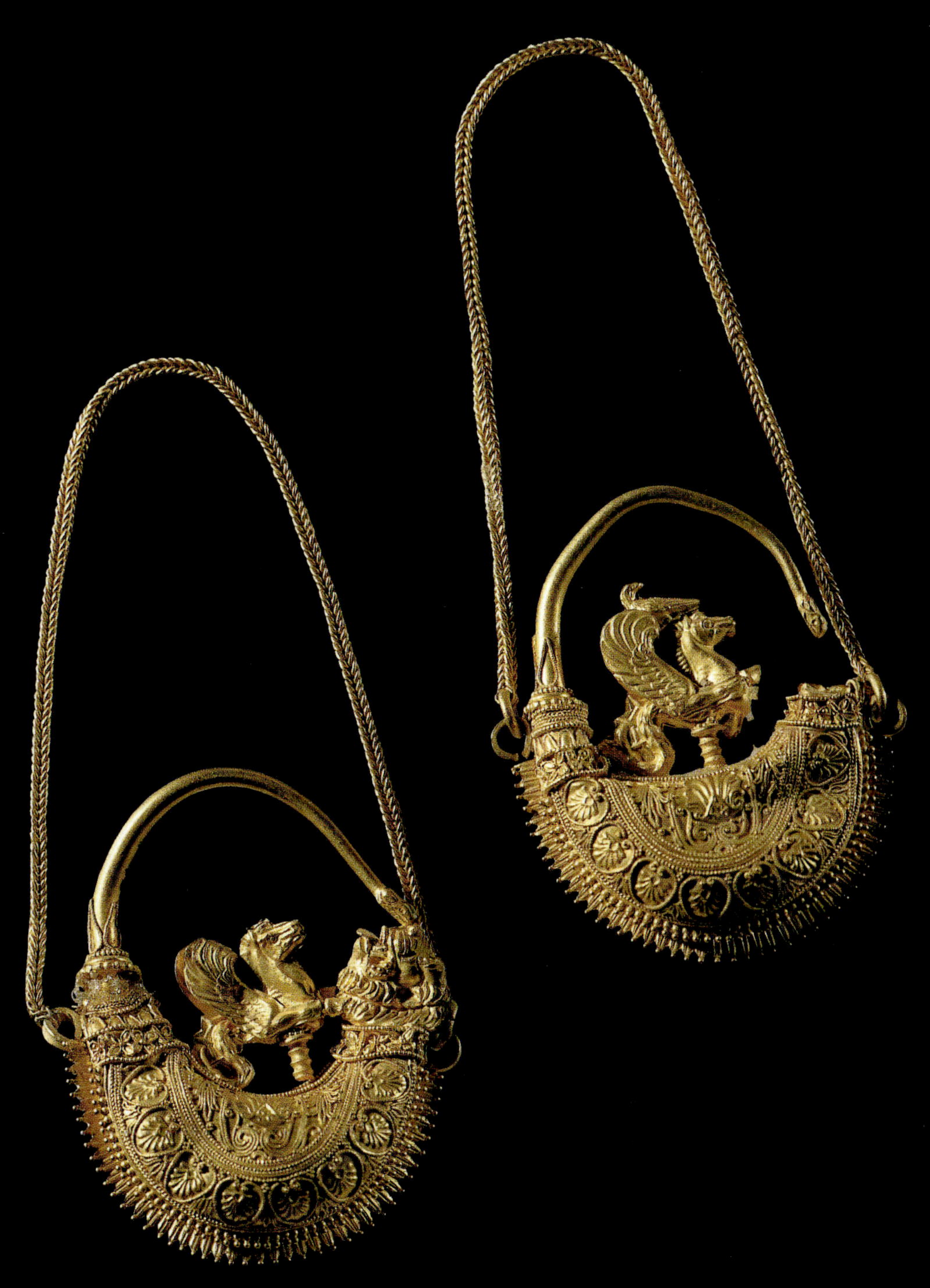

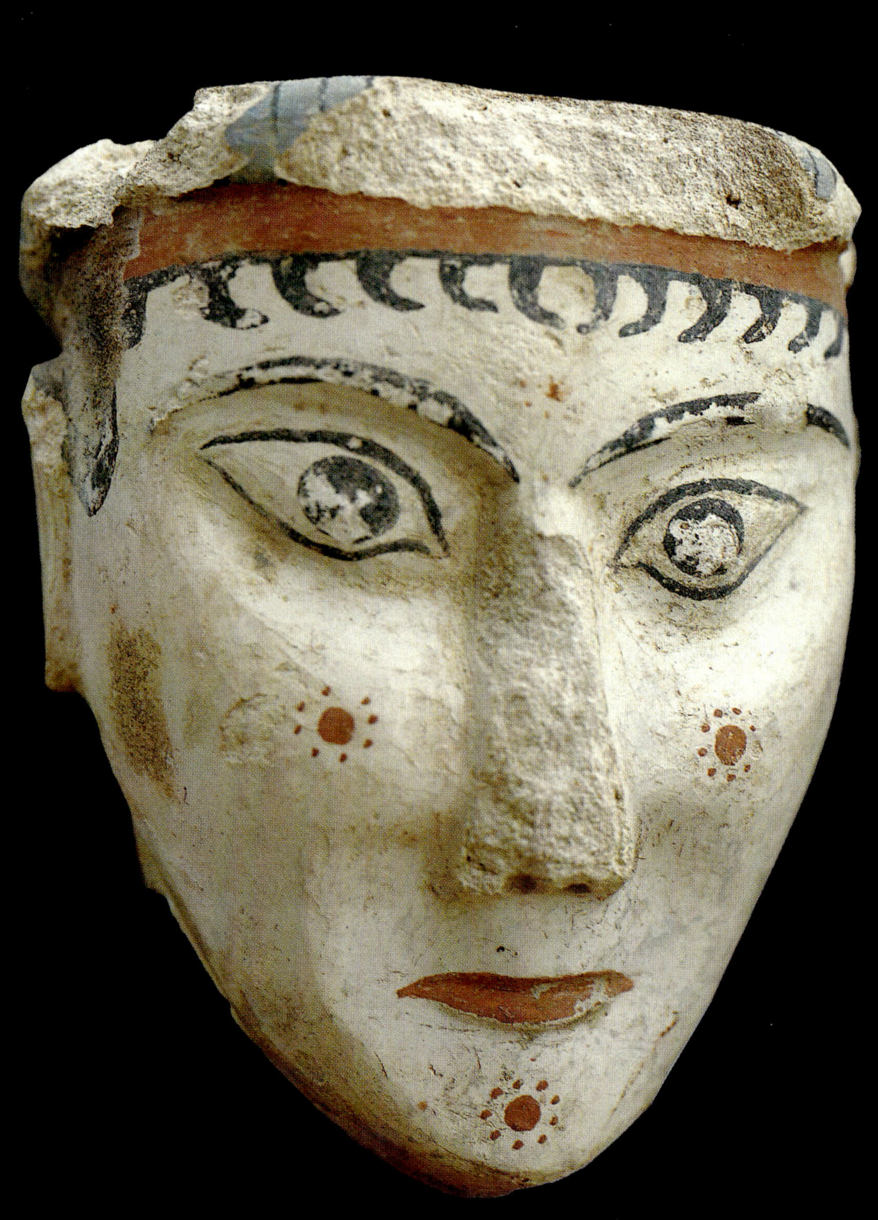

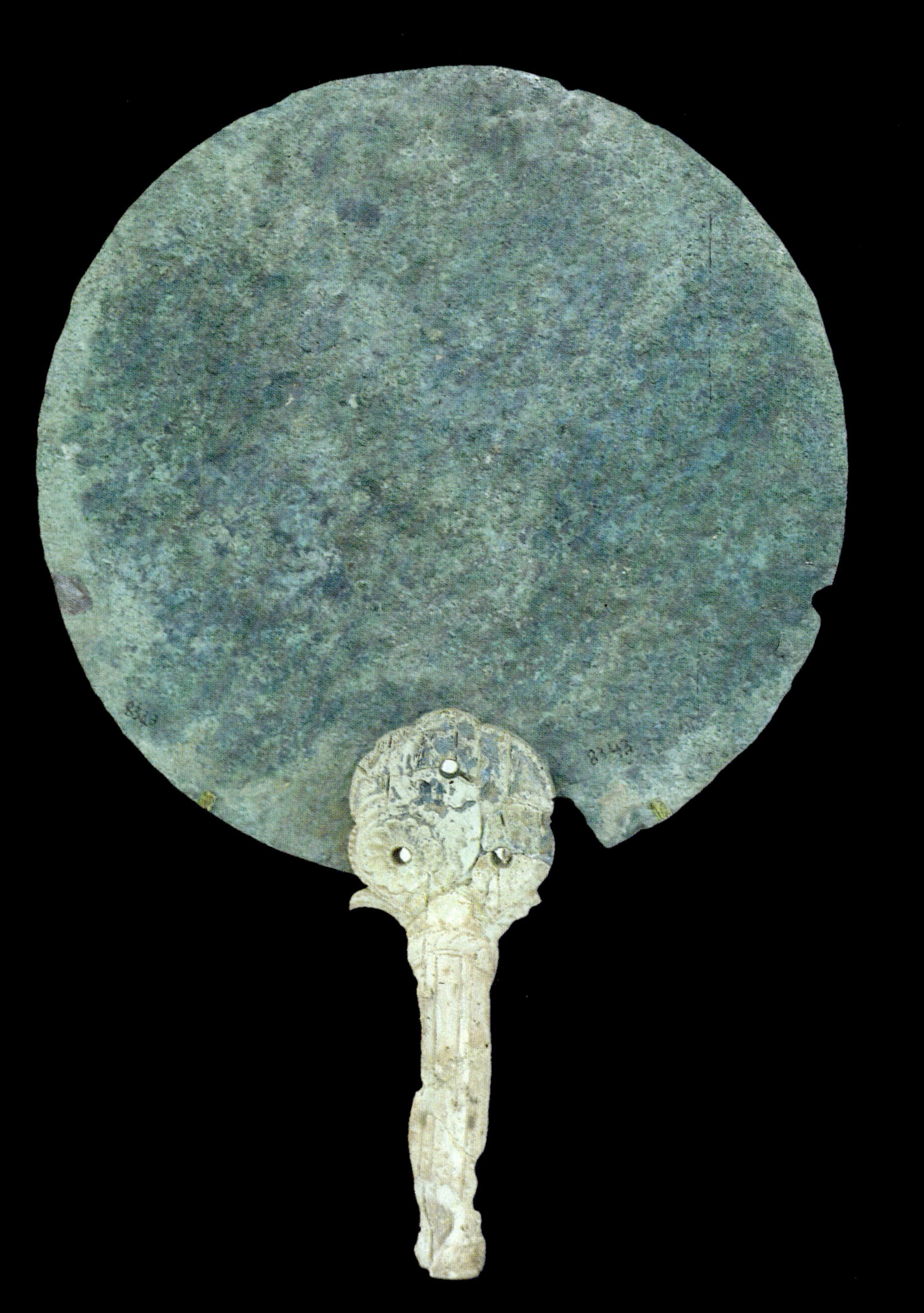

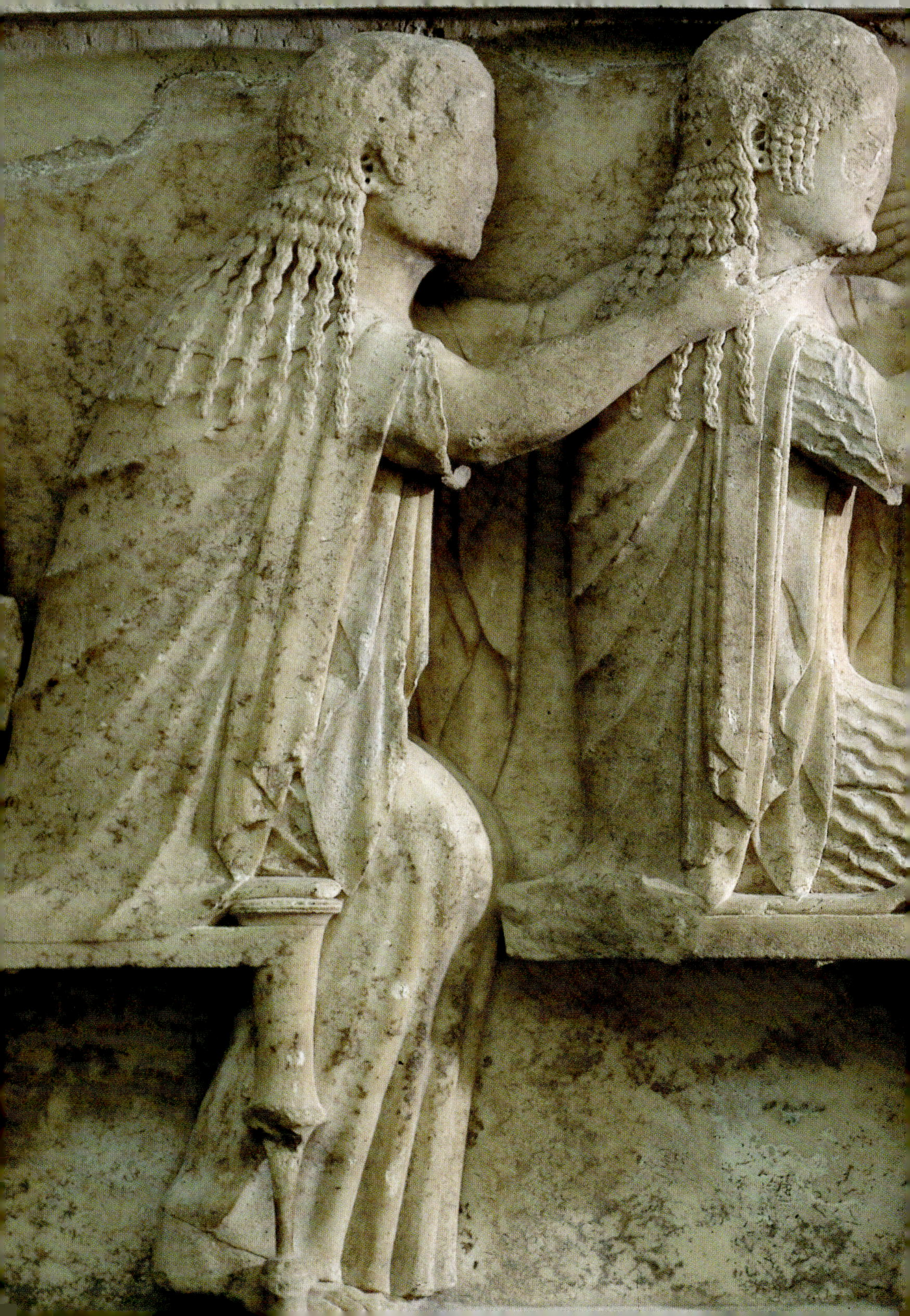

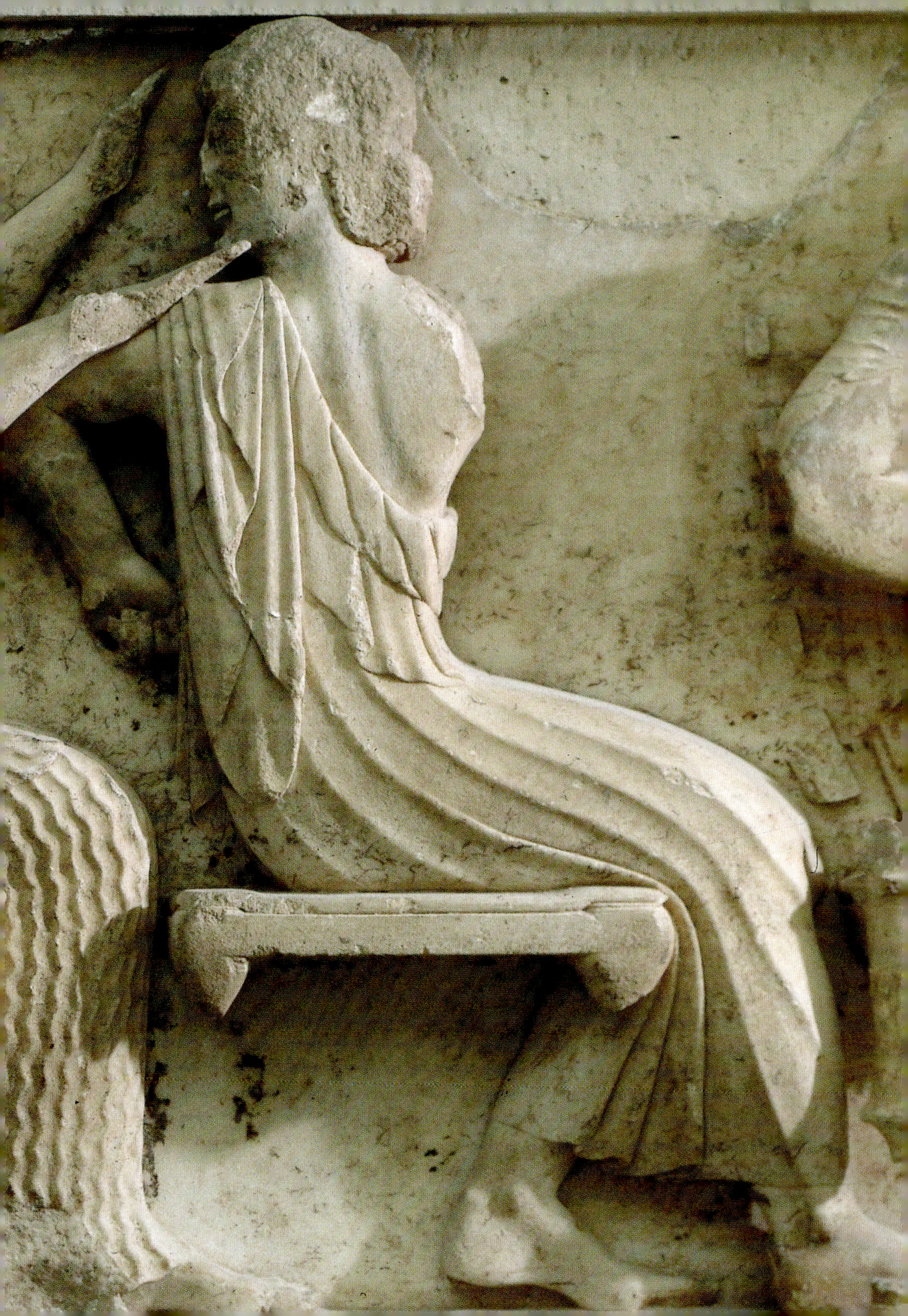

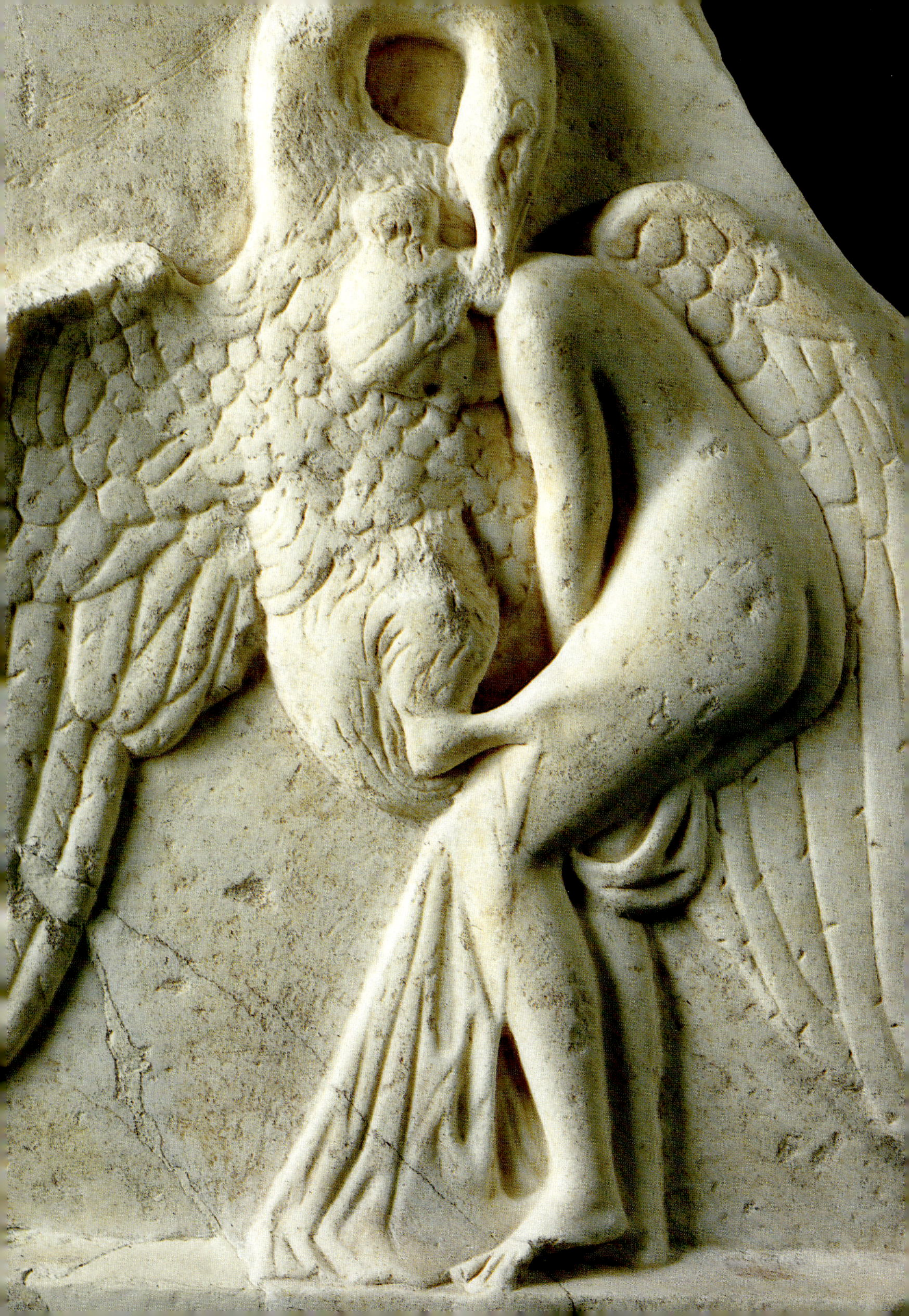

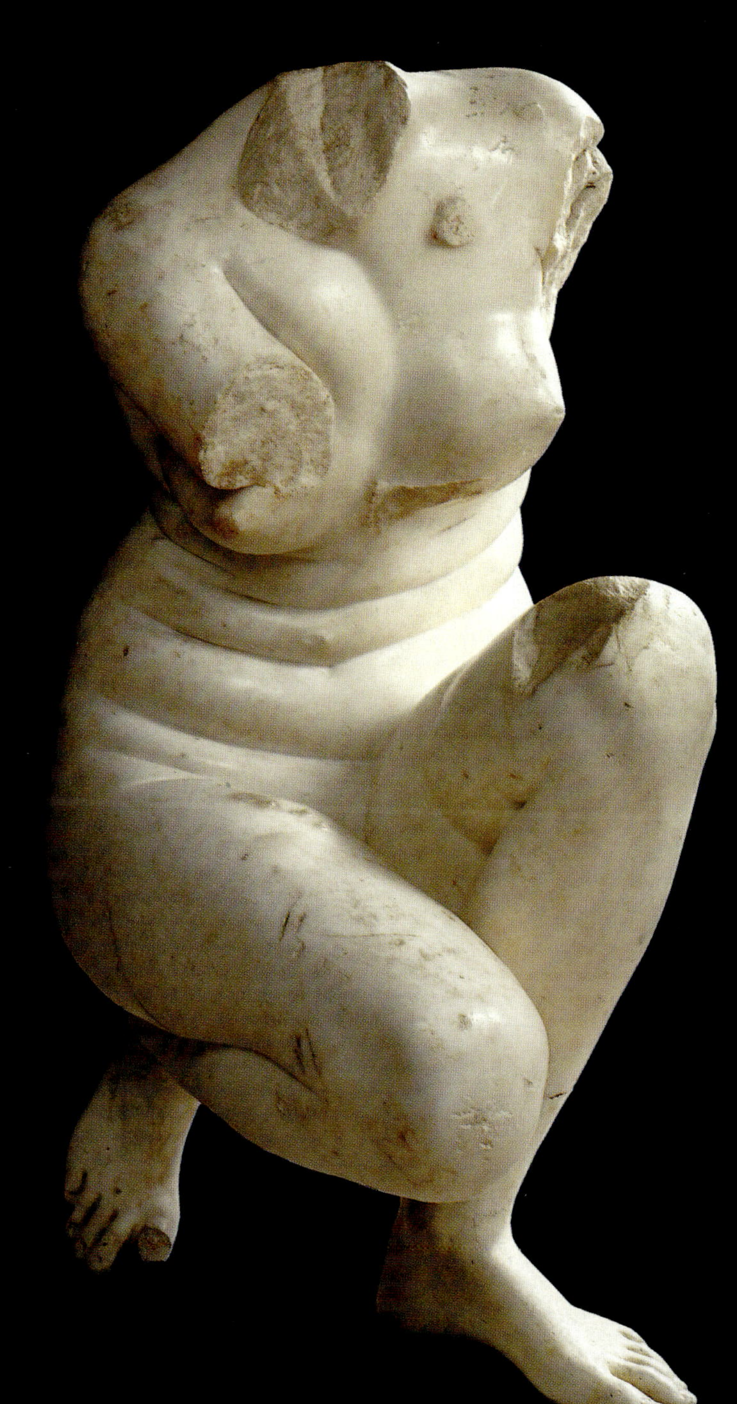

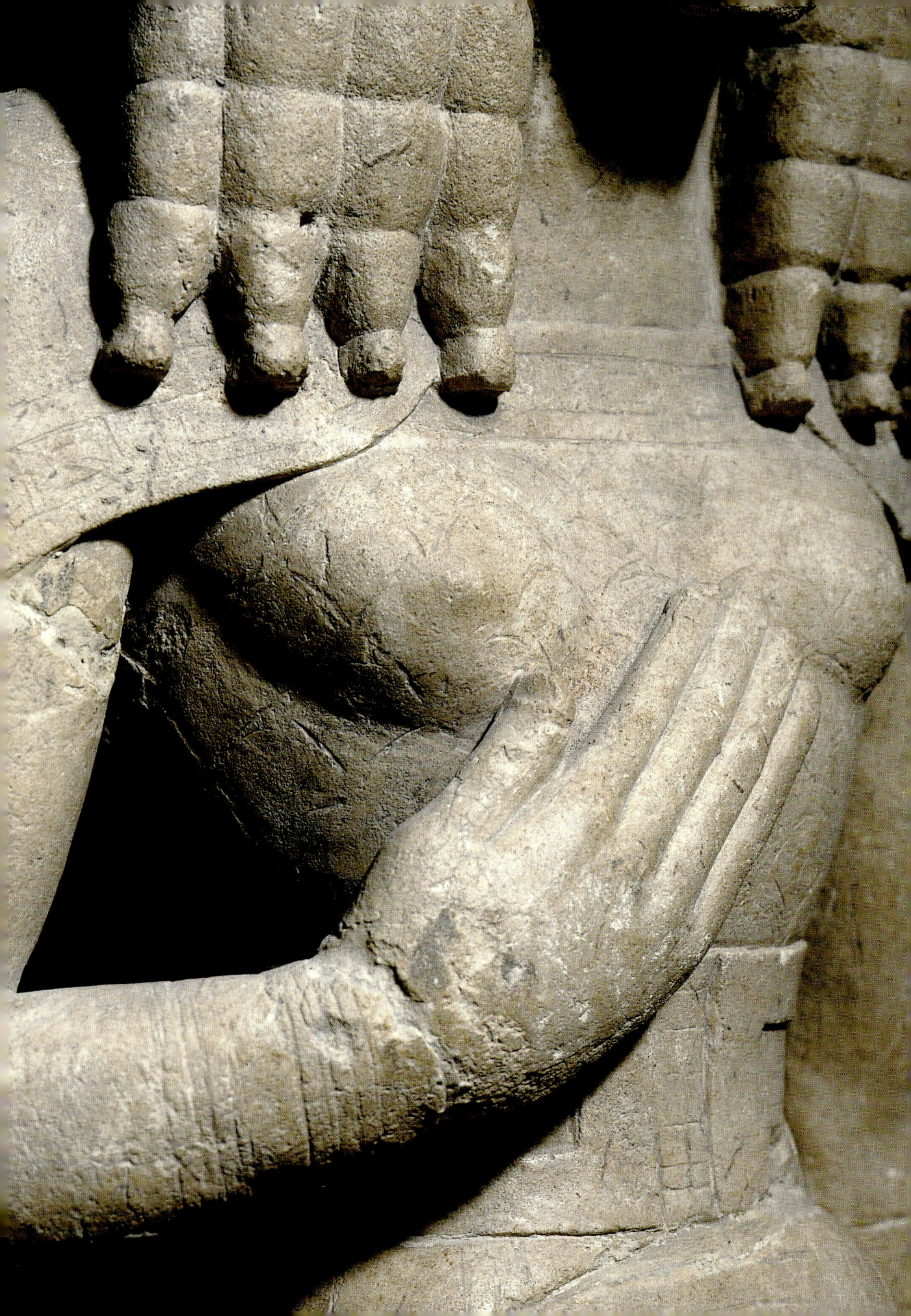

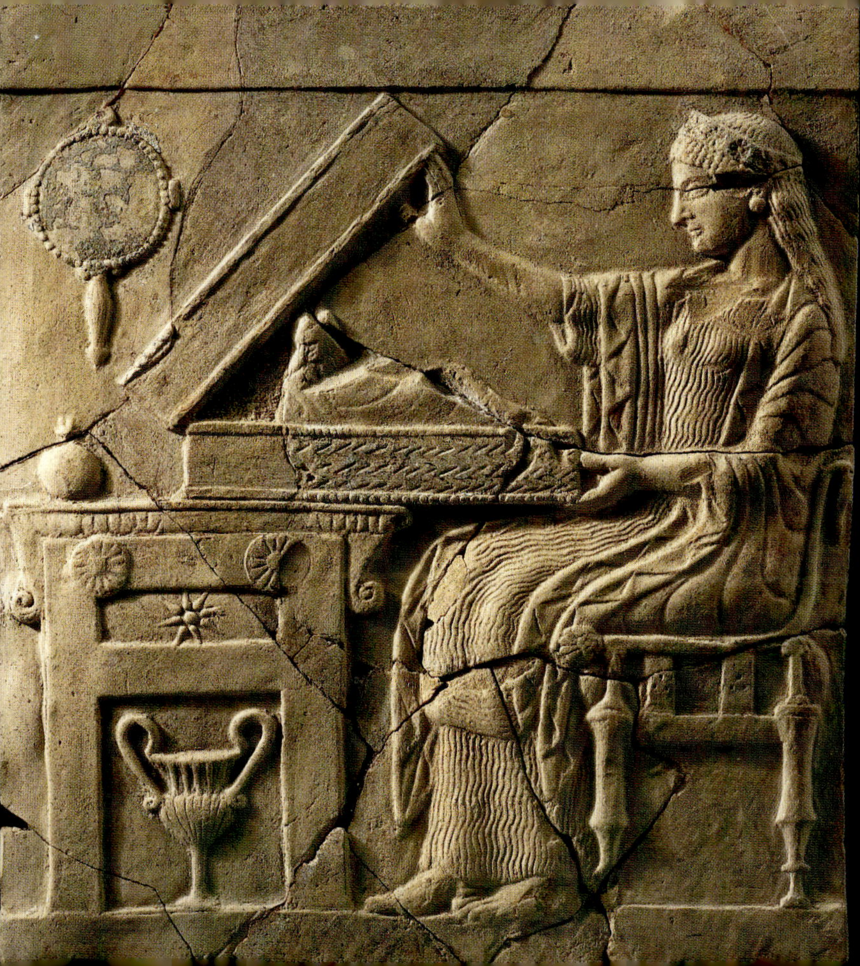

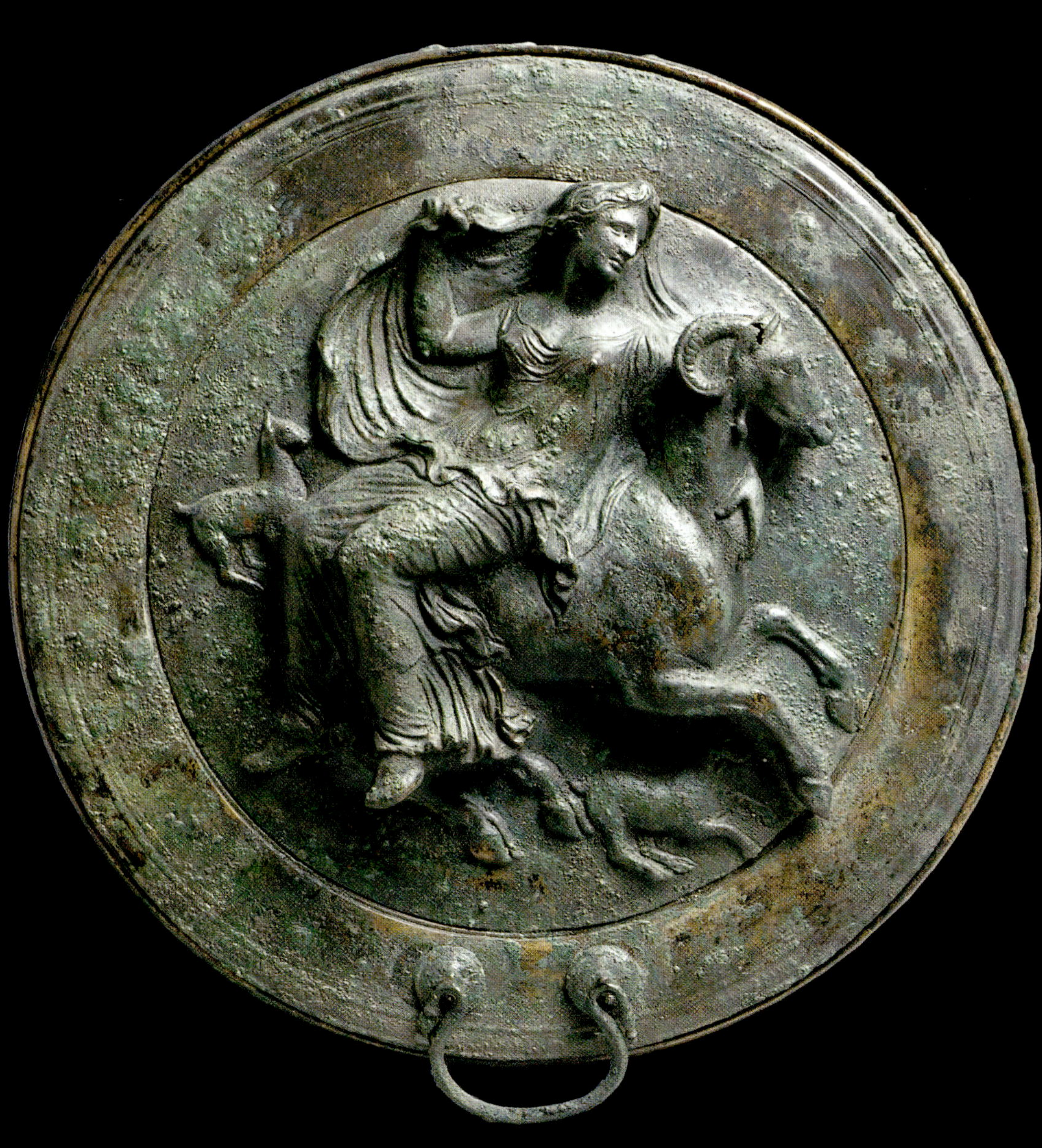

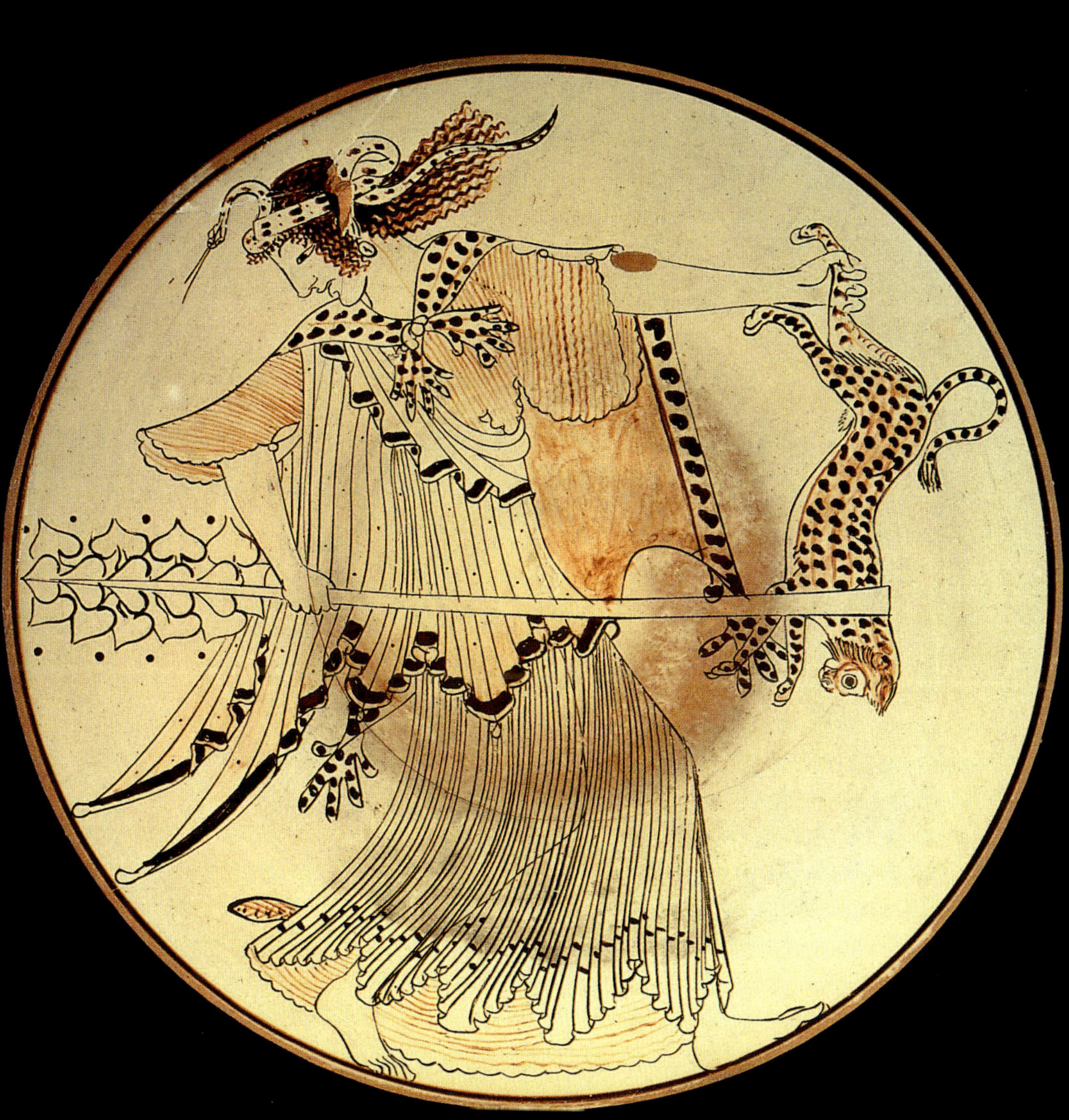

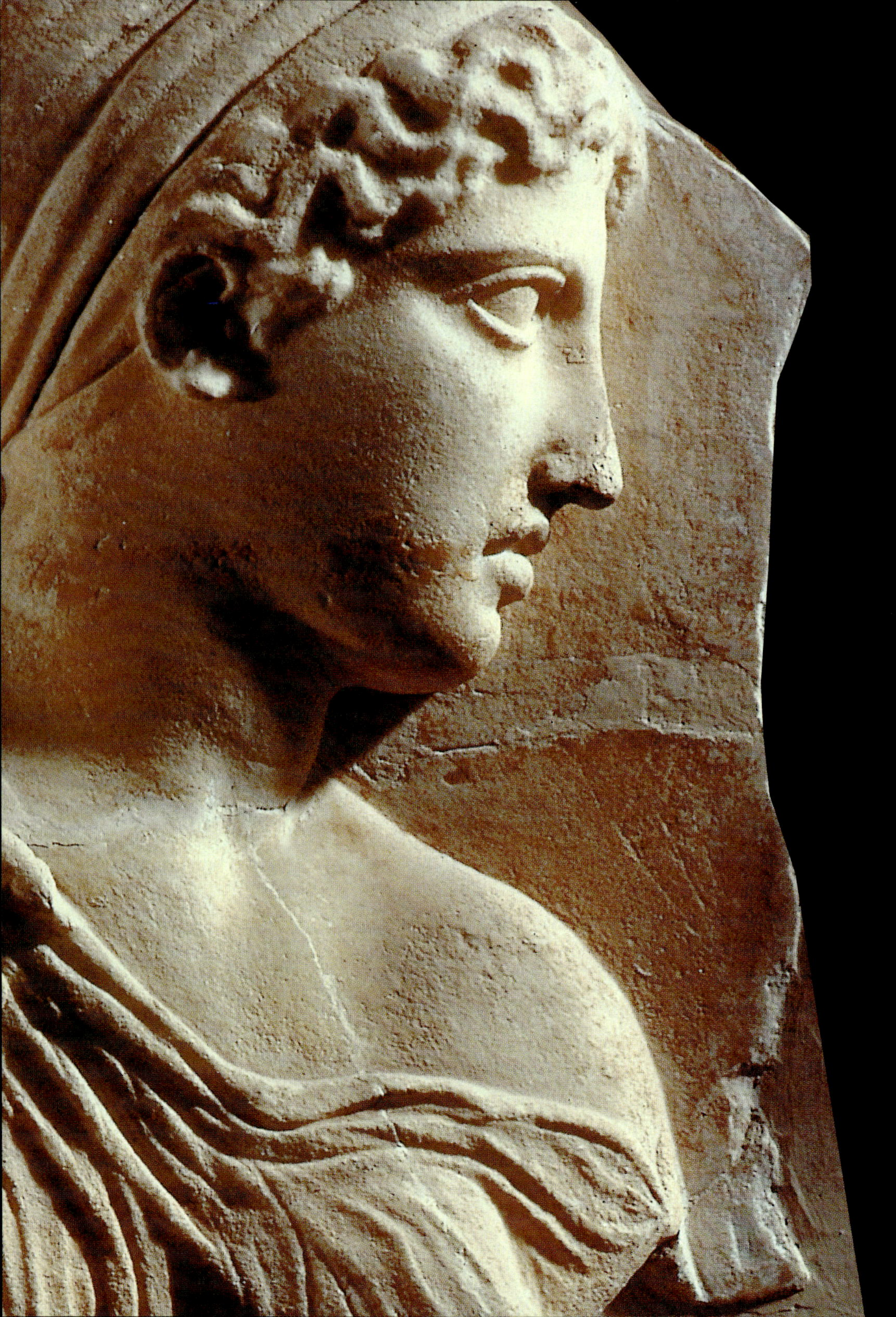

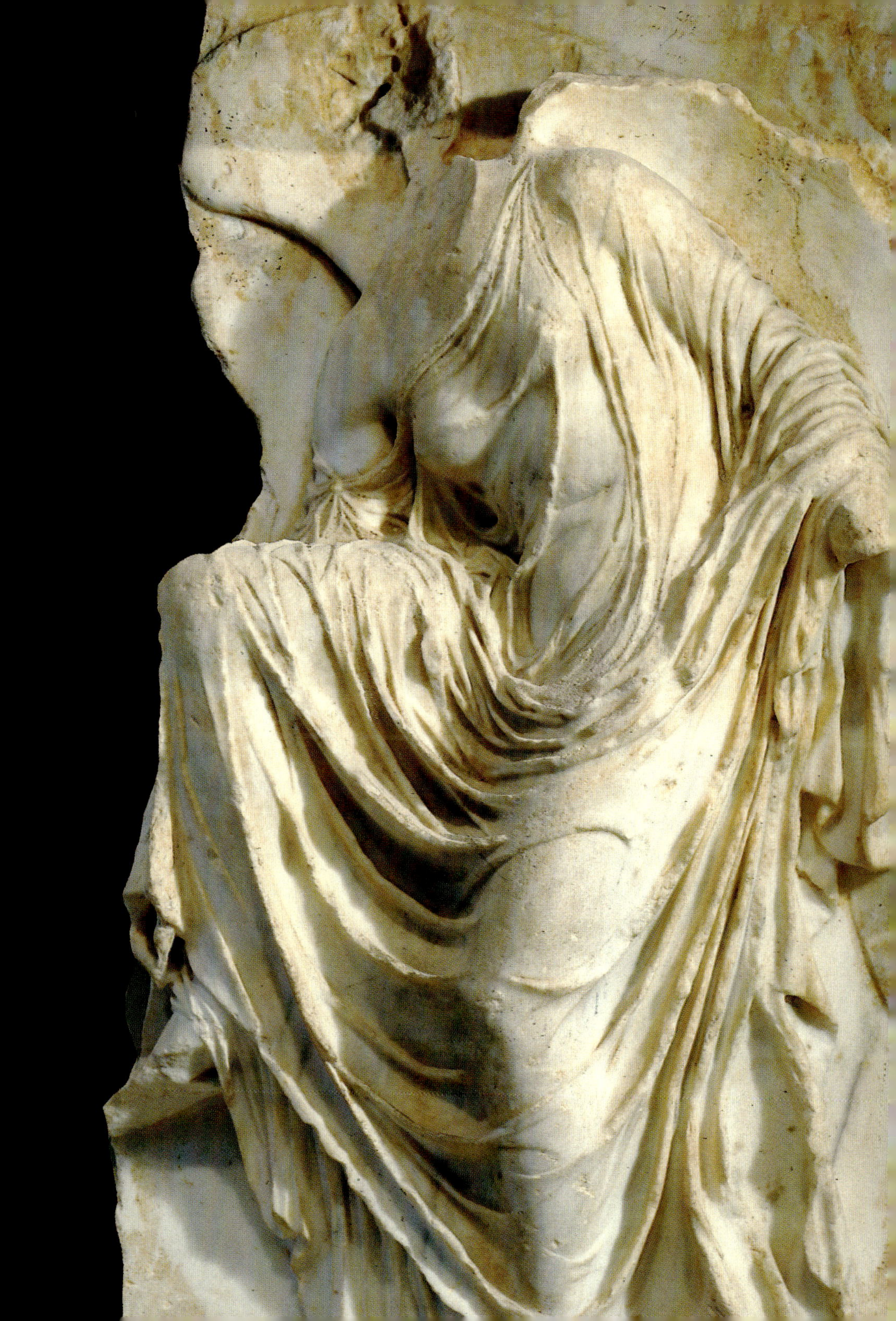

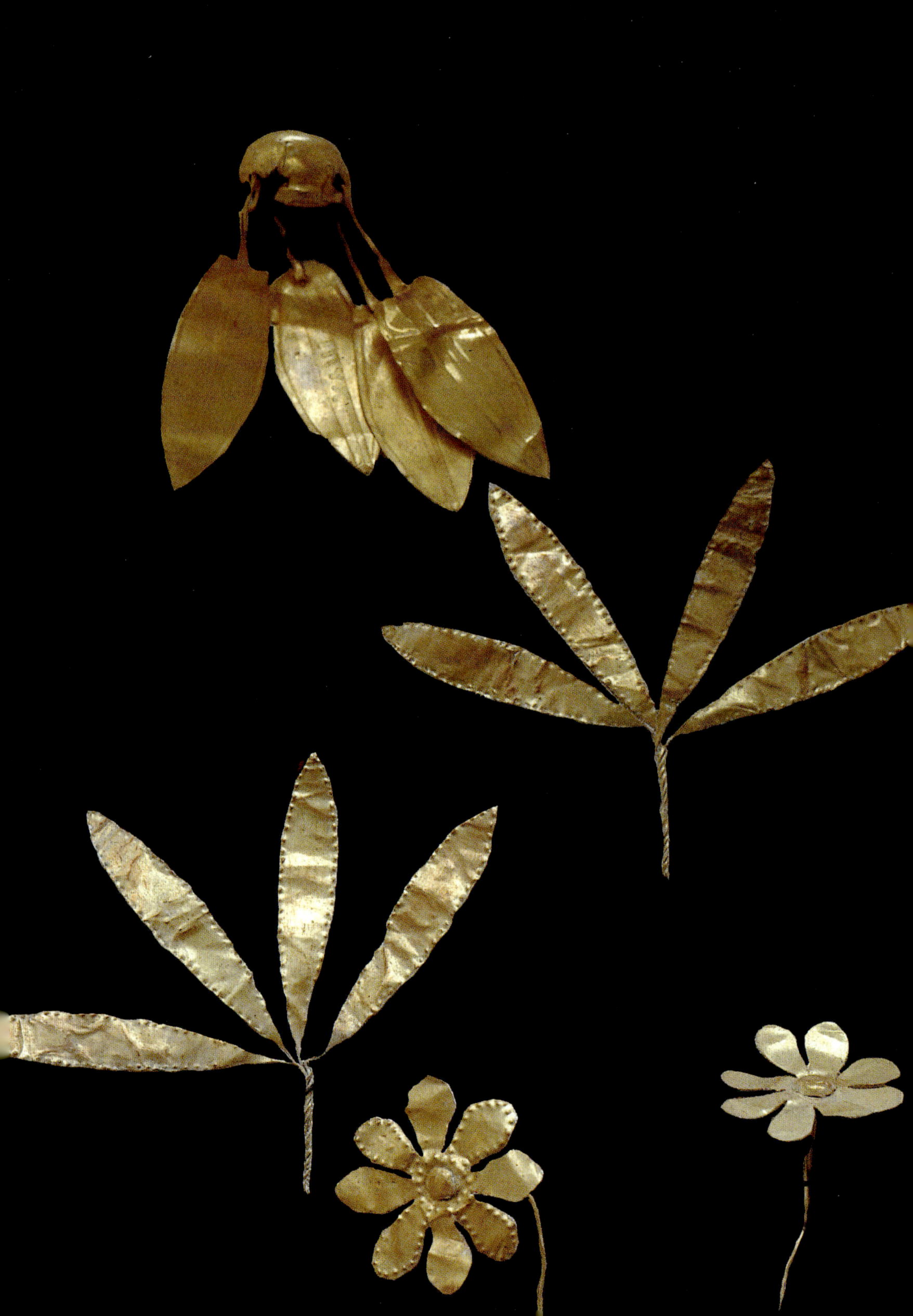

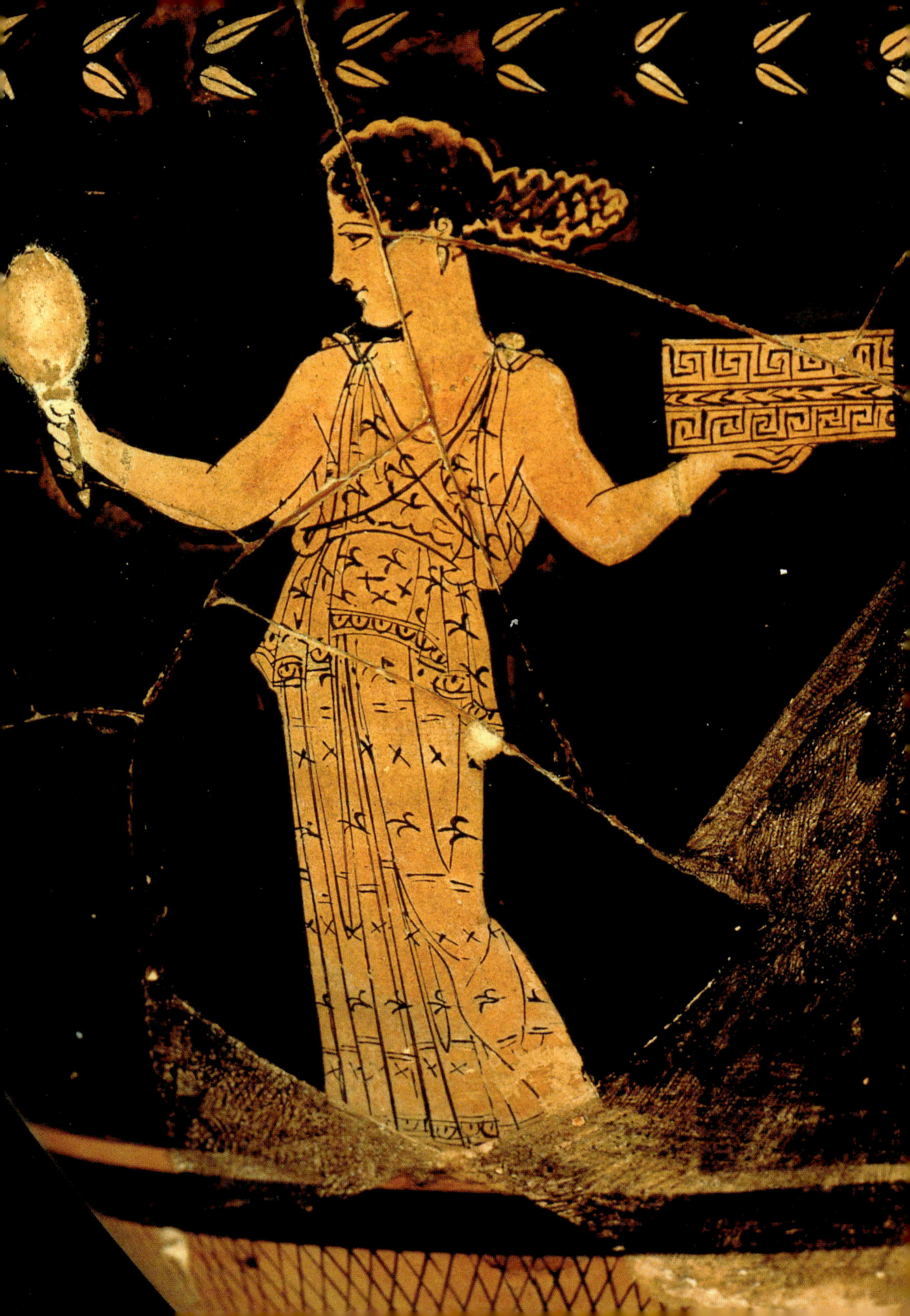

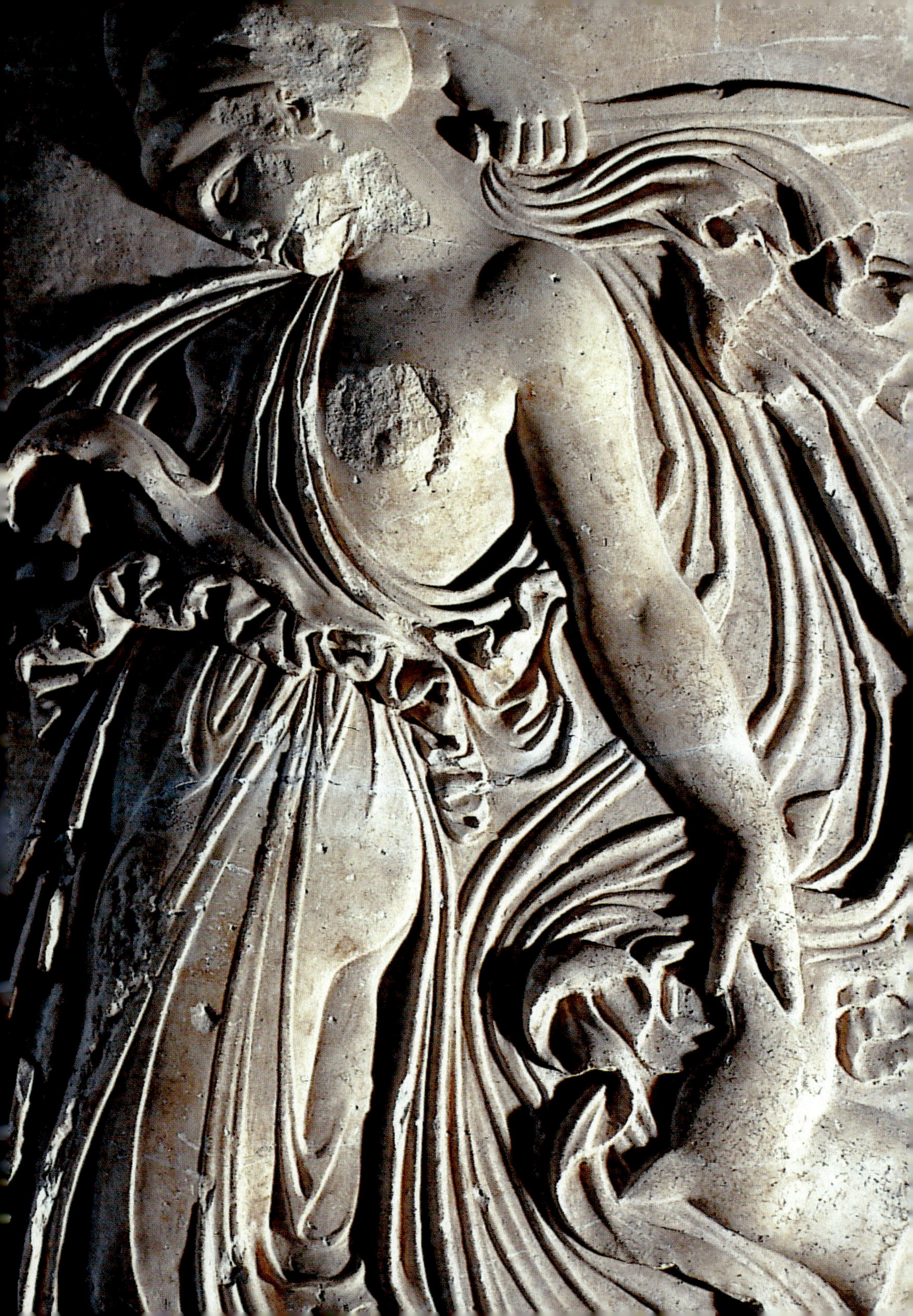

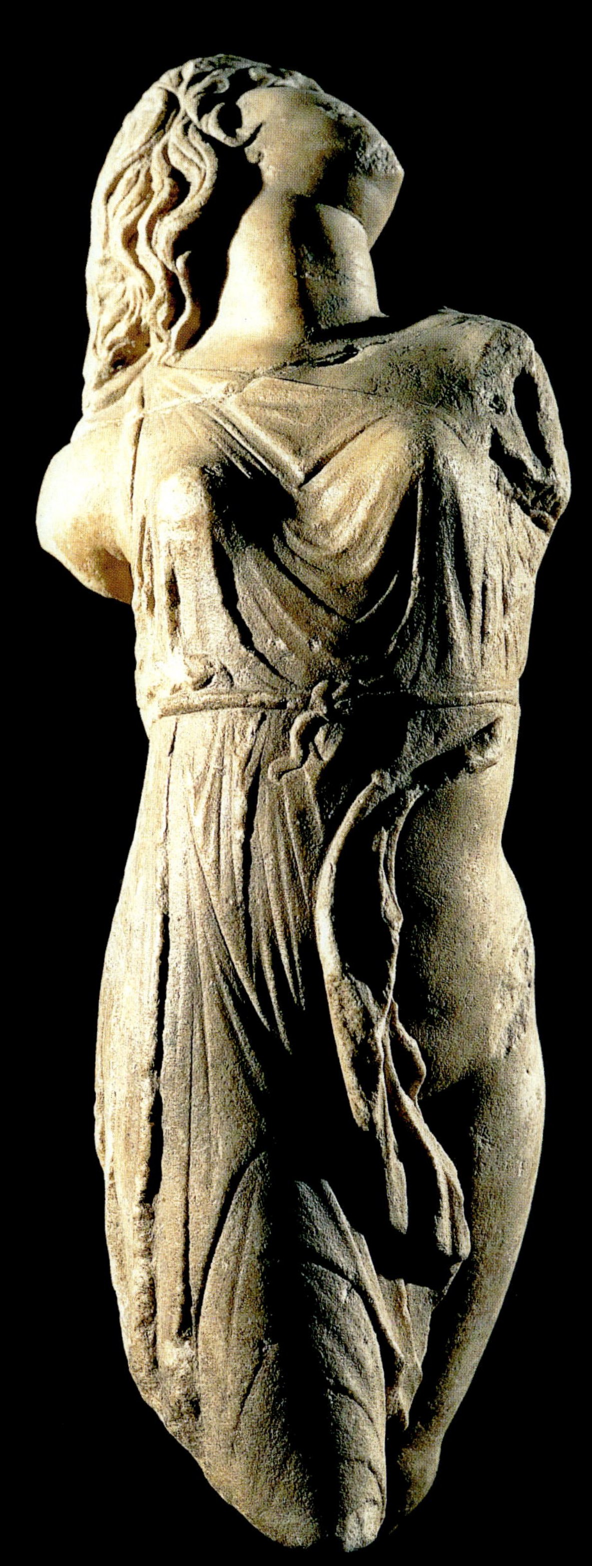

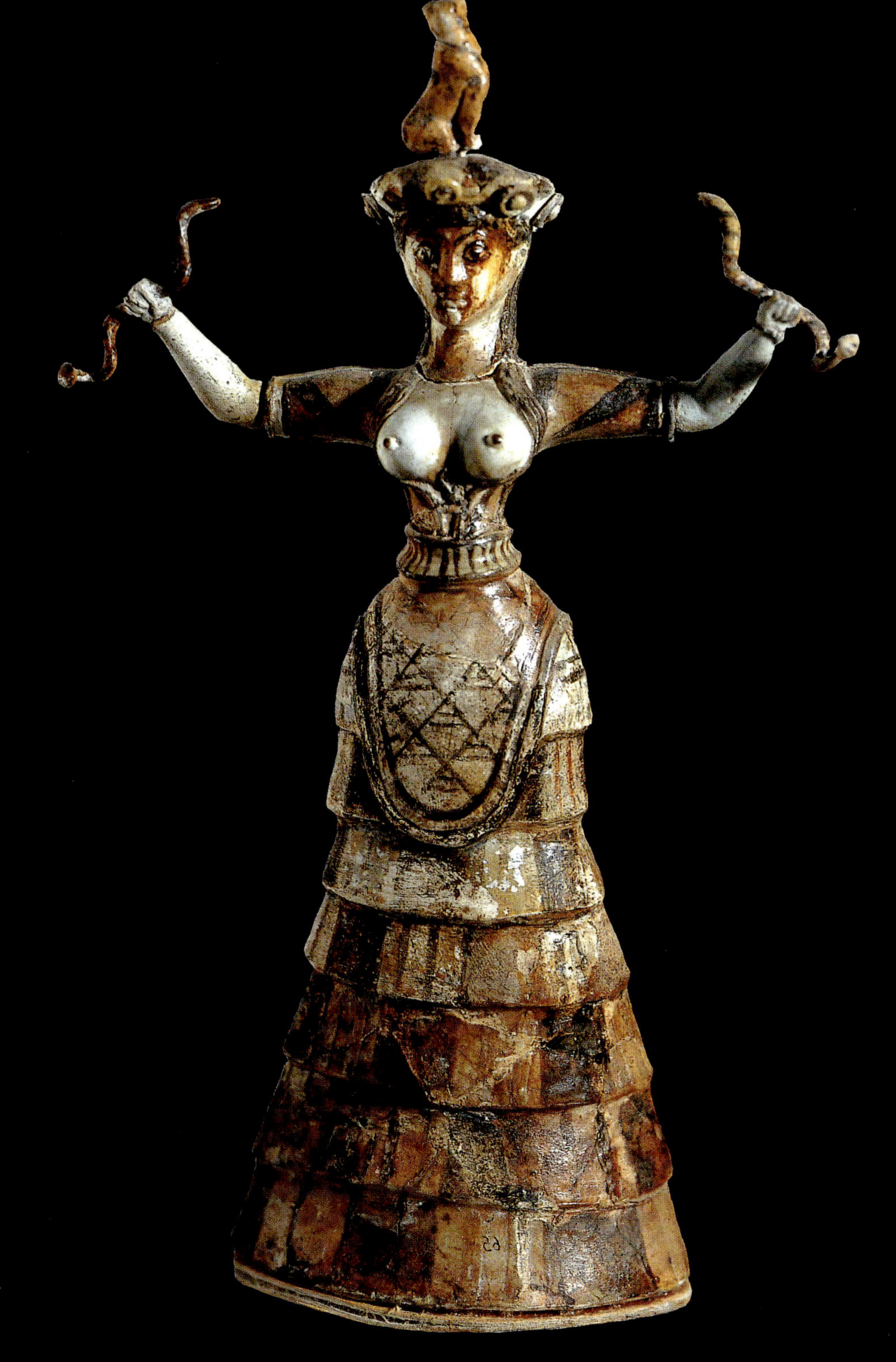

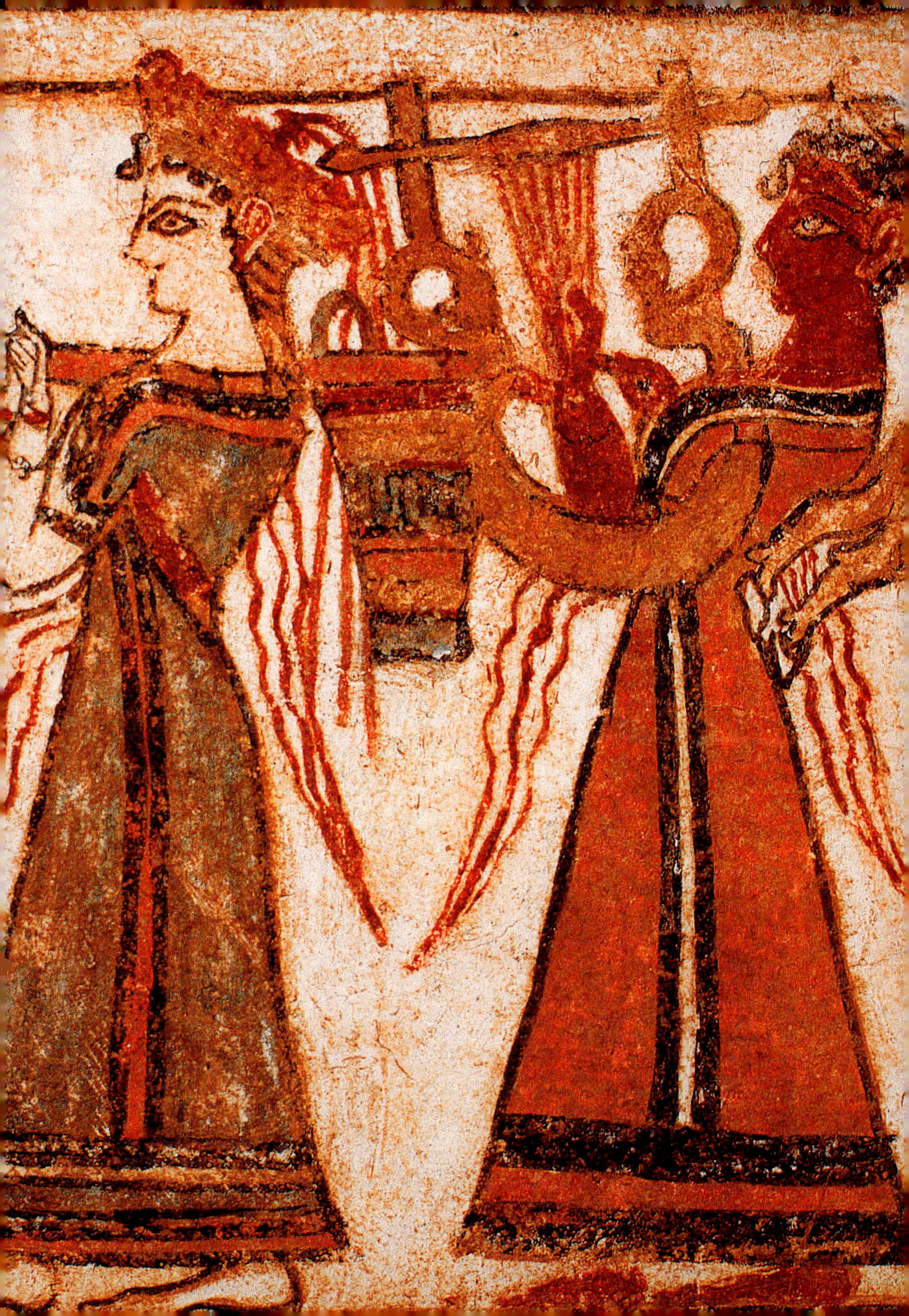

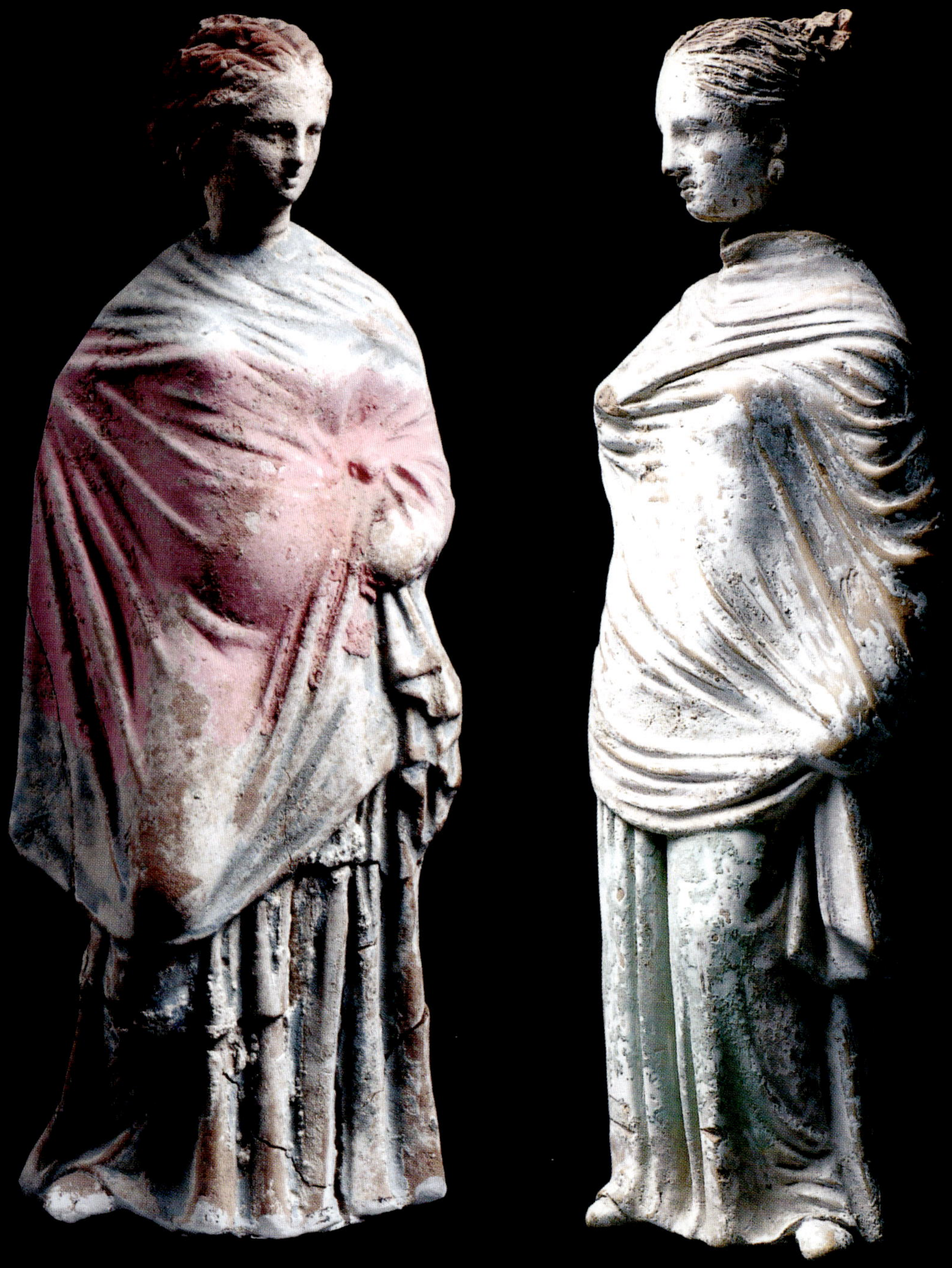

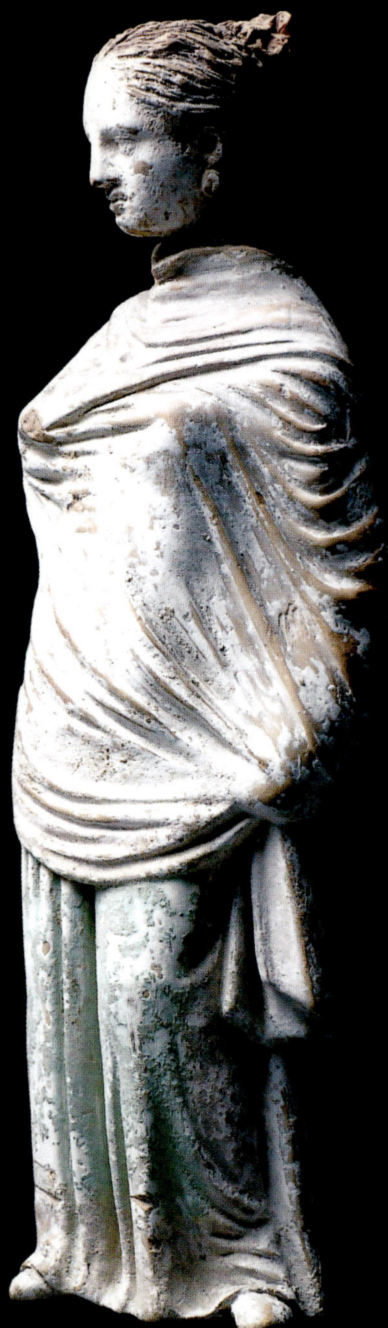

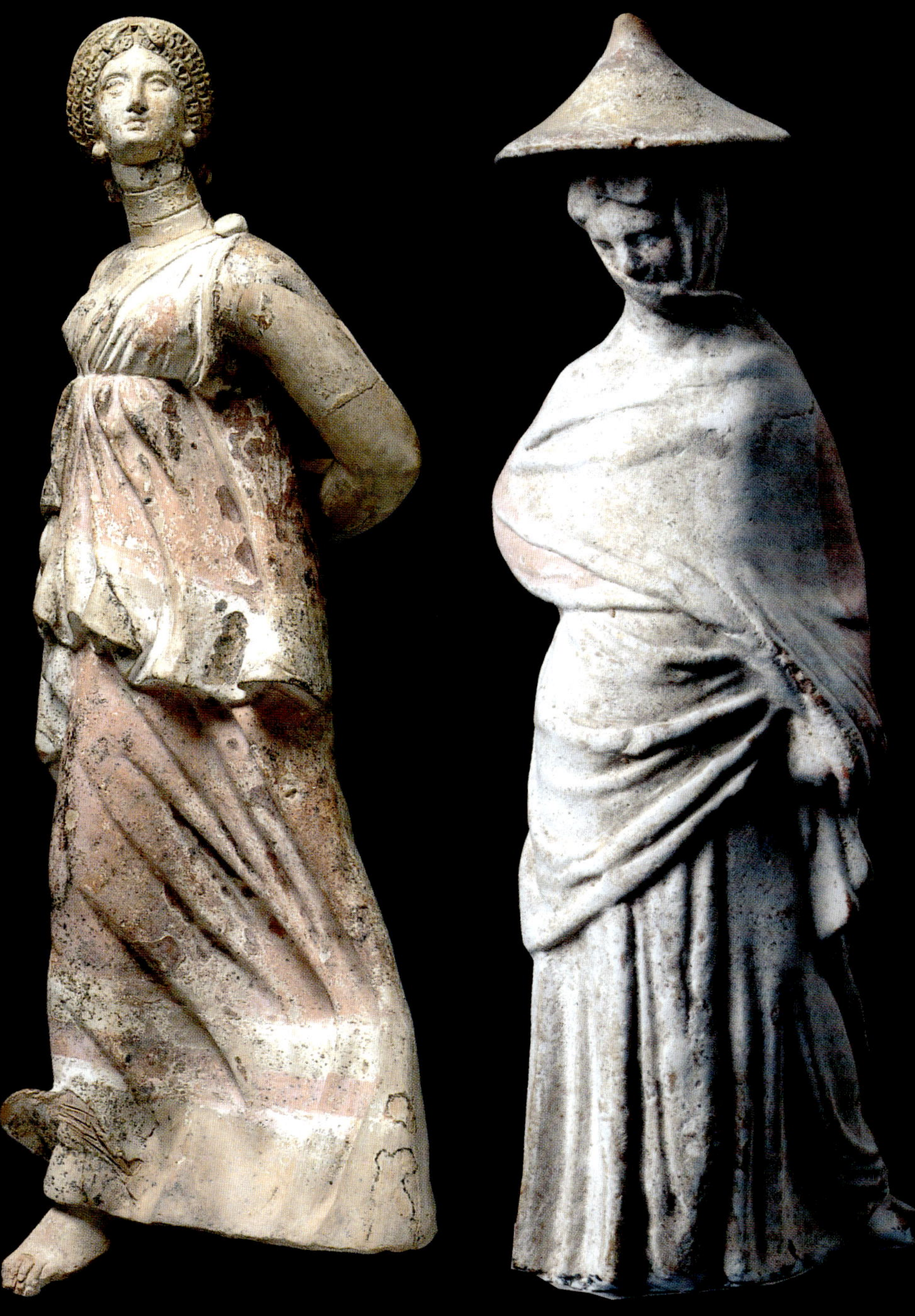

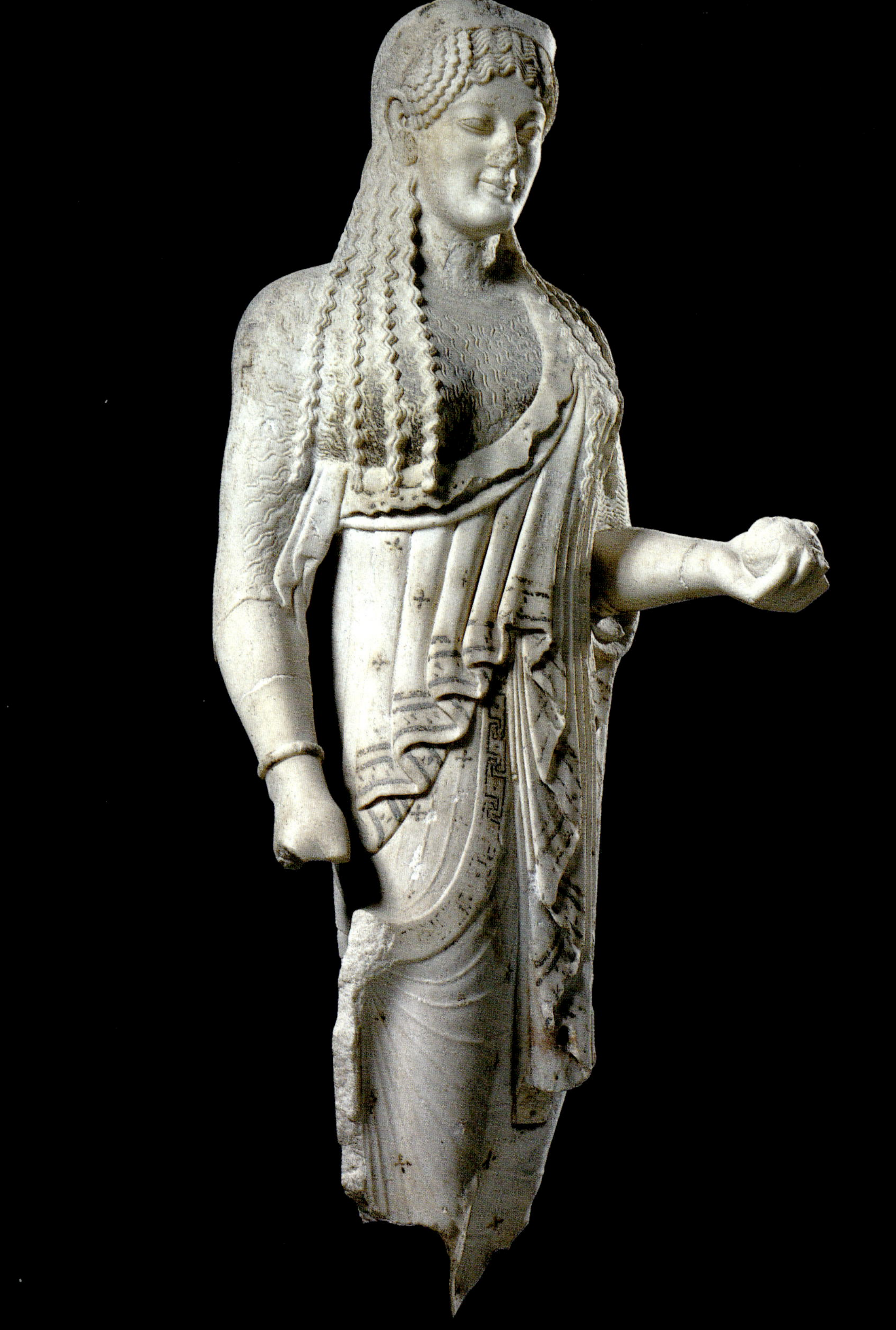

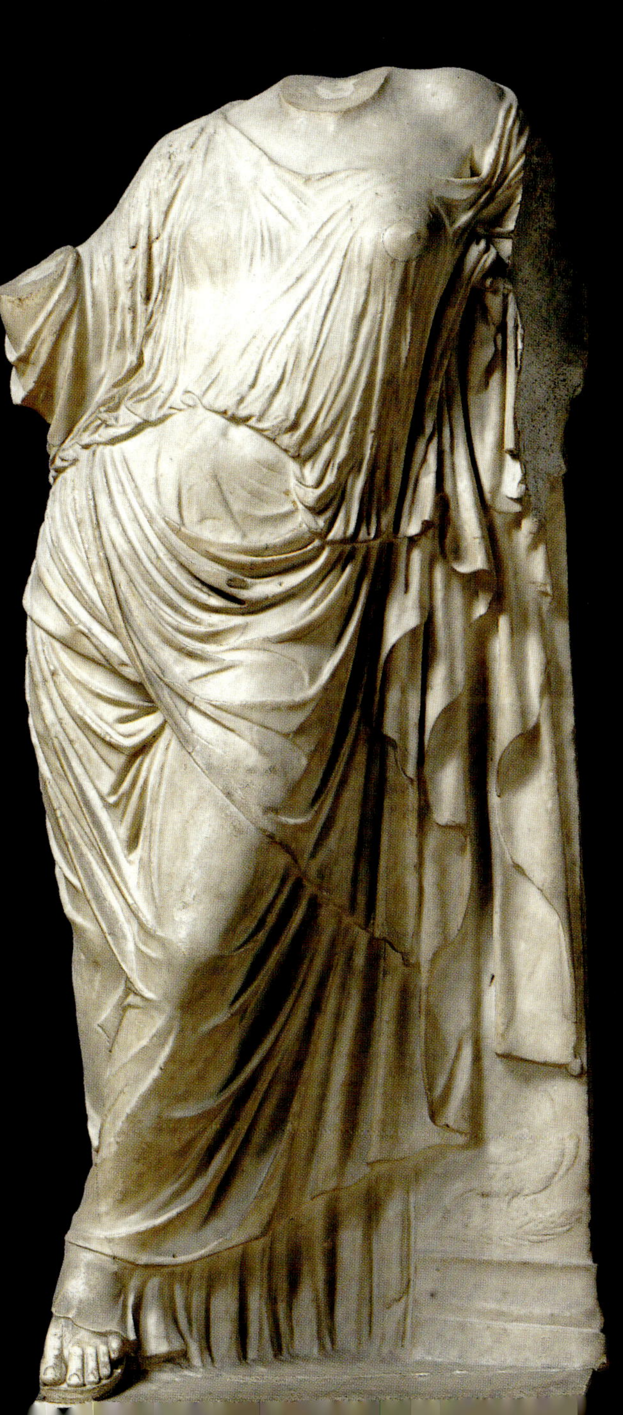

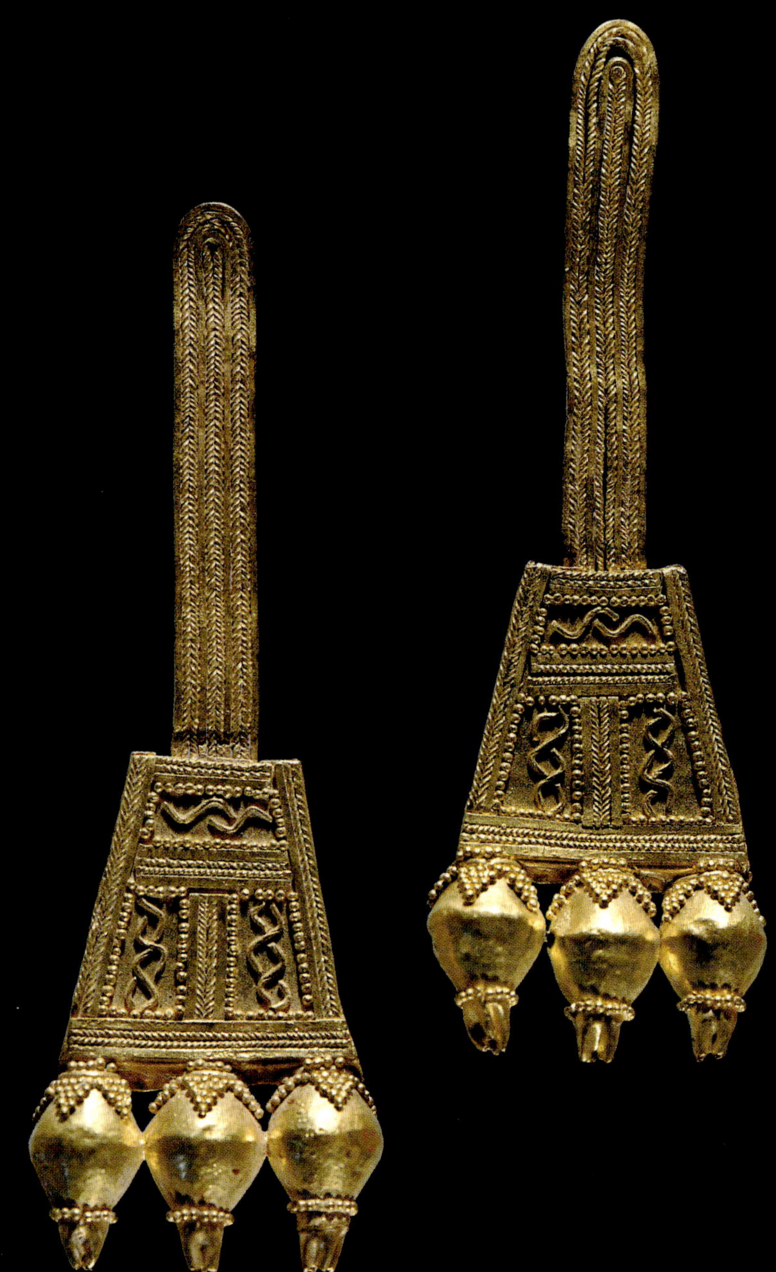

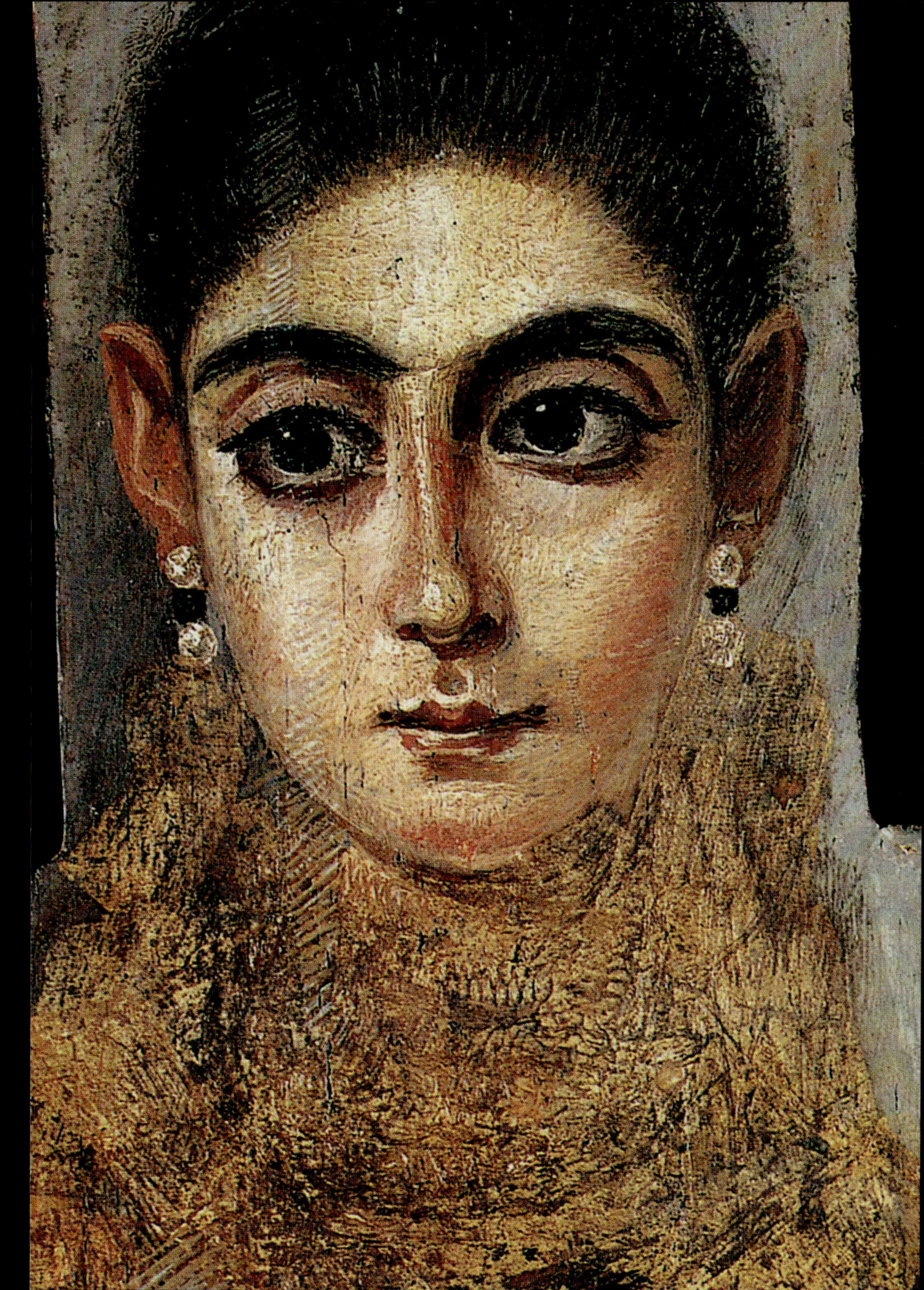

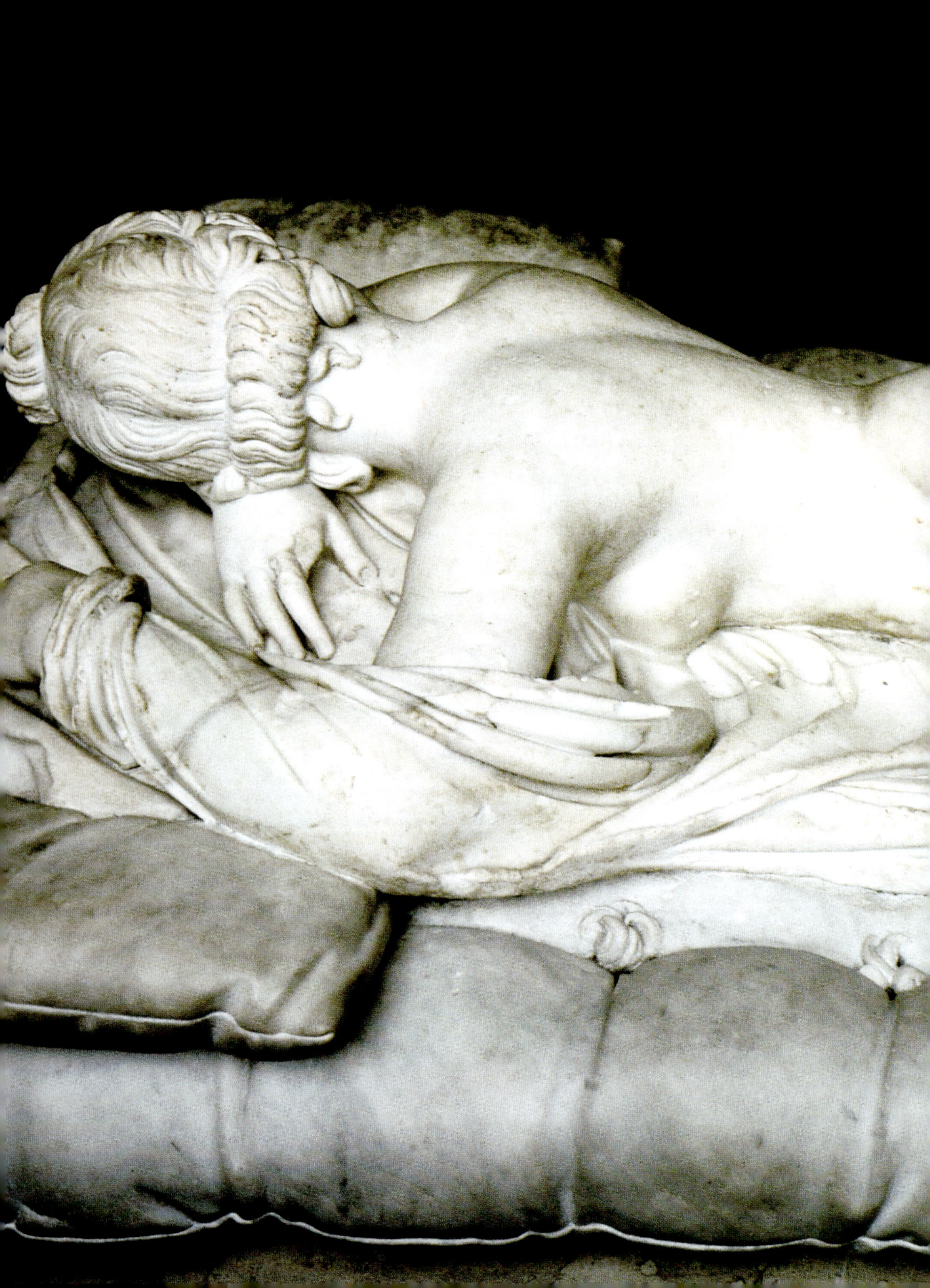

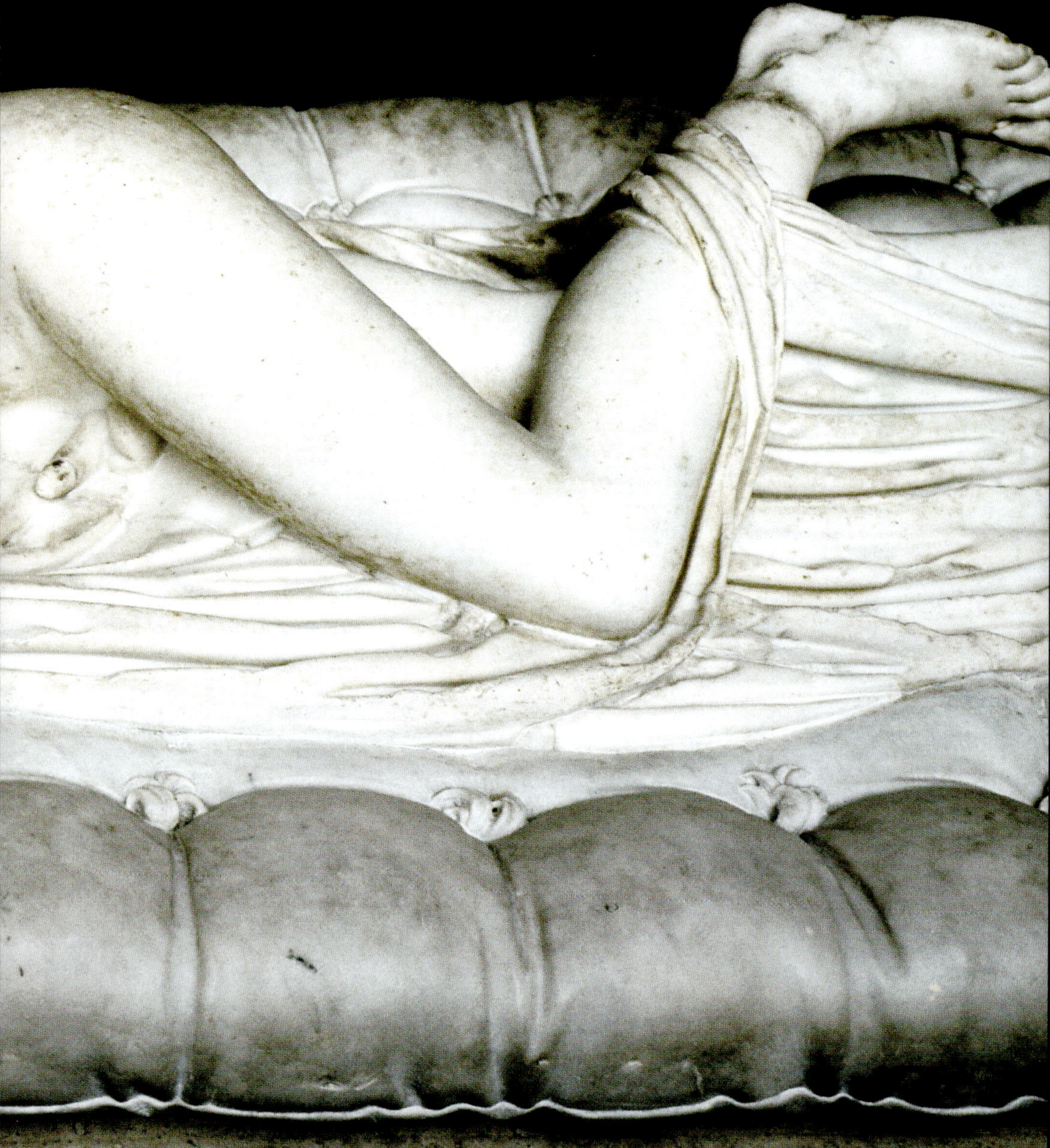

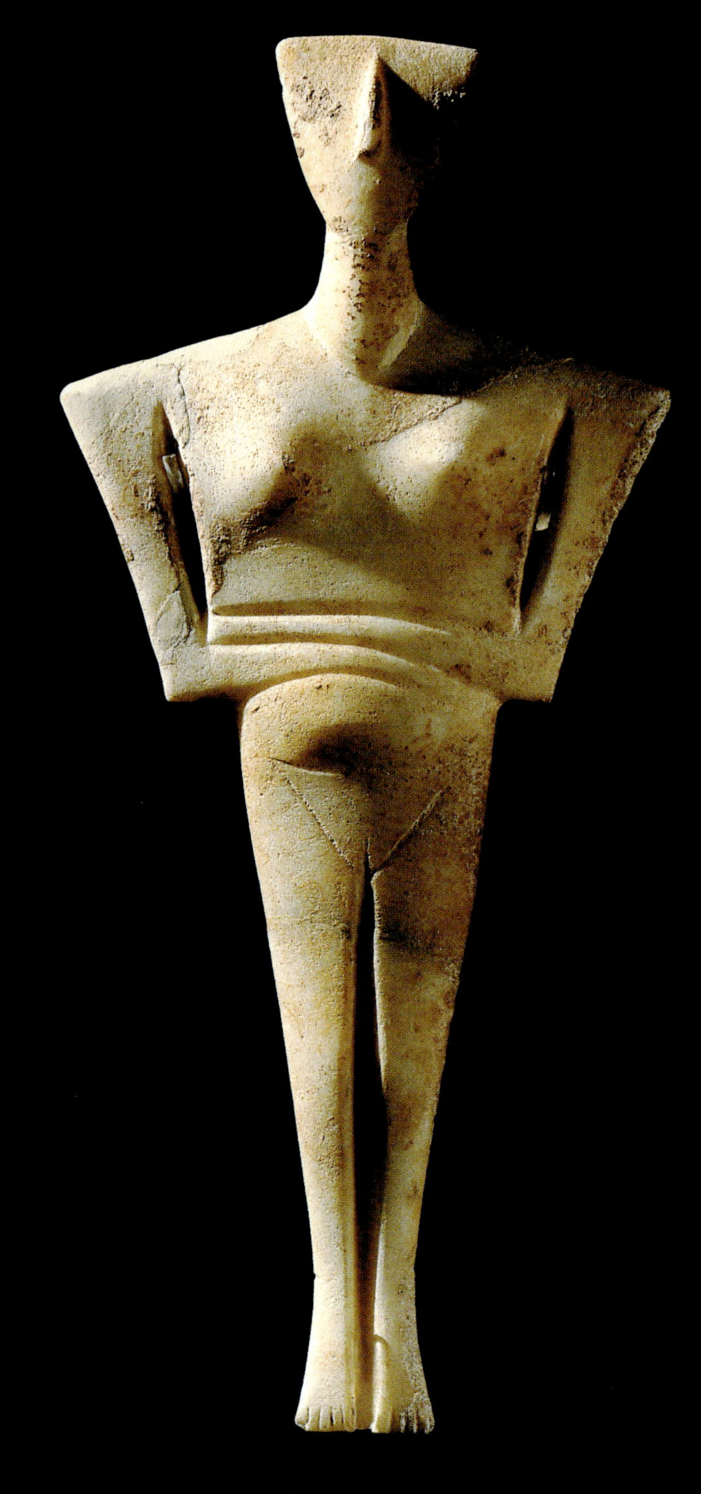

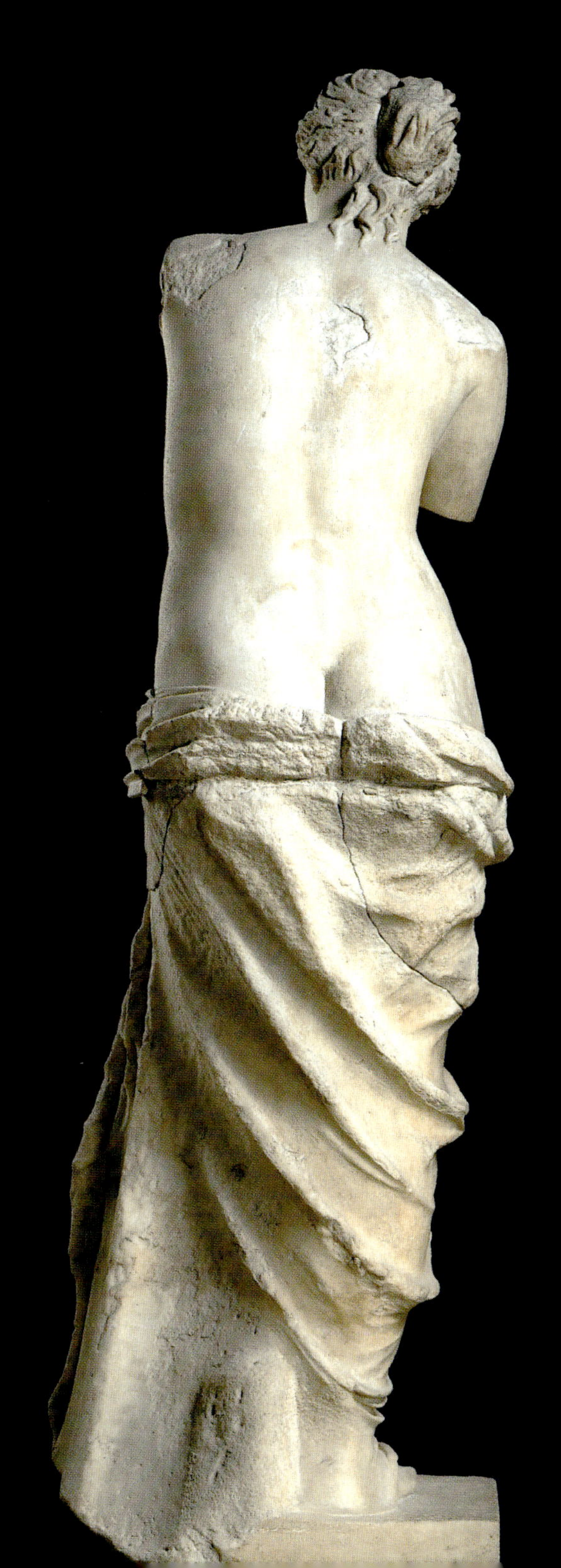

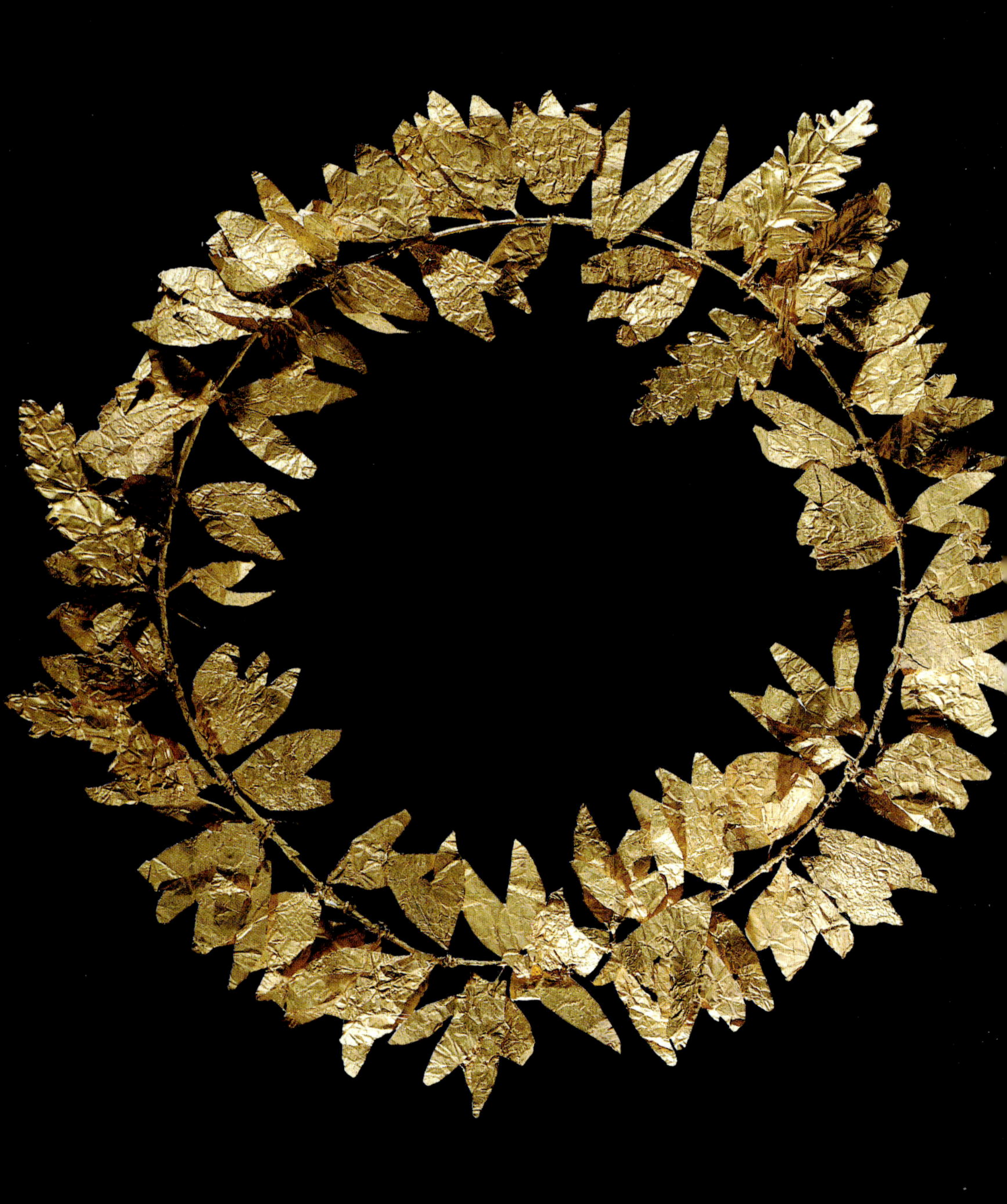

Greek Beauty: A Chronology

c. 3200–2800 B.C.: First violin-shaped idols from the Cyclades.

c. 2800–2300 B.C.: Golden age of the Cycladic idols, with arms crossed above the stomach to indicate fertility.

c. 2100–1750 B.C.: Middle Minoan period, first Cretan palaces at Knossos and Phaistos.

c. 1600 B.C.: Fresco known as "La Parisienne," Minoan art, palace at Knossos.

1500 B.C.: Eruption of the volcano on the island of Thera.
Frescoes at Akrotíri.

1600–1100 B.C.: Mycenean period on the mainland, in Greece.
"Sphinx" head in painted stucco.
Fresco with "Lady of Mycenae."

c. 650 B.C.: Daedalic Greek art, the best example of which is the "Auxerre Goddess" in the Louvre.

6th century B.C.: Archaic art. Kouroi discovered on the Acropolis.

5th century B.C.: Triumph of Classicism.

447–432 B.C.: Construction of the Parthenon directed by Phidias.

End 5th century B.C.: Statue "Aphrodite with Pillar," the original of which is attributed to Alcamenes.

c. 360 B.C.: "Aphrodite of Arles" attributed to Praxiteles.
The goddess's bust is revealed for the first time.

c. 340 B.C.: "Aphrodite of Cnidus," by Praxiteles, who immortalized in marble the perfect body of his companion, the courtesan Phryne.

3rd century B.C.: "Crouching Aphrodite," the original of which would certainly have been in bronze. This well-endowed nude may well have been the work of a Greek sculptor from Asia Minor.

120–80 B.C.: "Venus de Milo," the most famous of Aphrodites from the Hellenistic

Laurel wreath, 4th–3rd century B.C. Gold. Museum, Volos. This gold wreath, with its ethereal lightness and grace, seems to be closely related to the diadems found in the tomb of Philip II at Vergina. © G. Dagli Orti, Paris.

Greek Beauty: A Bibliography

Selected bibliography:

BLUNDELL, Sue. *Women in Ancient Greece.* Cambridge, Mass.: Harvard University Press, 1995.

BOARDMAN, John. *Greek Sculpture: The Archaic Period.* London: Thames & Hudson, 1985.

BOARDMAN, John. *Greek Sculpture: The Classical Period.* London: Thames & Hudson, 1985.

BOARDMAN, John. *The History of Greek Vases.* London: Thames & Hudson, 2001.

CARPENTER, Thomas. *Art and Myth in Ancient Greece.* London: Thames and Hudson, 1991.

CHARBONNEAUX, Jean. *Archaic Greek Art.* New York: G. Braziller, 1971.

COARELLI, Filippo. *Greek and Roman Jewelry.* London: The Hamlyn Publishing Group Limited, 1966.

FANTHAM, Elaine, Helene Peet FOLEY, Natalie Boymel KAMPEN, Sarah B. POMEROY, H. Alan HIGGINS, Reynold Alleyne. *Greek and Roman Jewelry.* University of California Press, Los Angeles: 1980.

PEDLEY, John G. *Greek Art and Archaeology.* Englewood Cliffs: Prentice Hall, 2002.

SCHEFOLD, Karl. *Myth and Legend in Early Greek Art.* New York: Abrams, 1966.

SHAPIRO. *Women in the Classical World: Image and Text.* Oxford: Oxford University Press, 1994.

SYMONS, David J. *Costume of Ancient Greece.* New York: Chelsea House Publishers, 1987.

ZINSERLING, Verena. *Women in Greece and Rome.* New York: Abner Schram, 1973.

Sources:

ARISTOPHANES. *Lysistrata.* Project Gutenberg (http://promo.net/pg/).

EURIPIDES. *The Bacchantes.* Internet Classics (http://classics.mit.edu).

HOMER. *The Iliad.* Translated by Samuel Butler. Internet Classics (http://classics.mit.edu).

SAPPHO. Translated by D. W. Myatt (http://classicpersuasion.org/pw/sappho/sappmyatt.htm).

Portrait of a Young Woman (Sappho): *The Poet of Pompeii, 1st century. Polychrome fresco, Pompeii. Museo Archeologico Nazionale, Naples. This refined portrait illustrates the Pompeiians' liking for Greek literature.* © Lessing/AKG Paris.

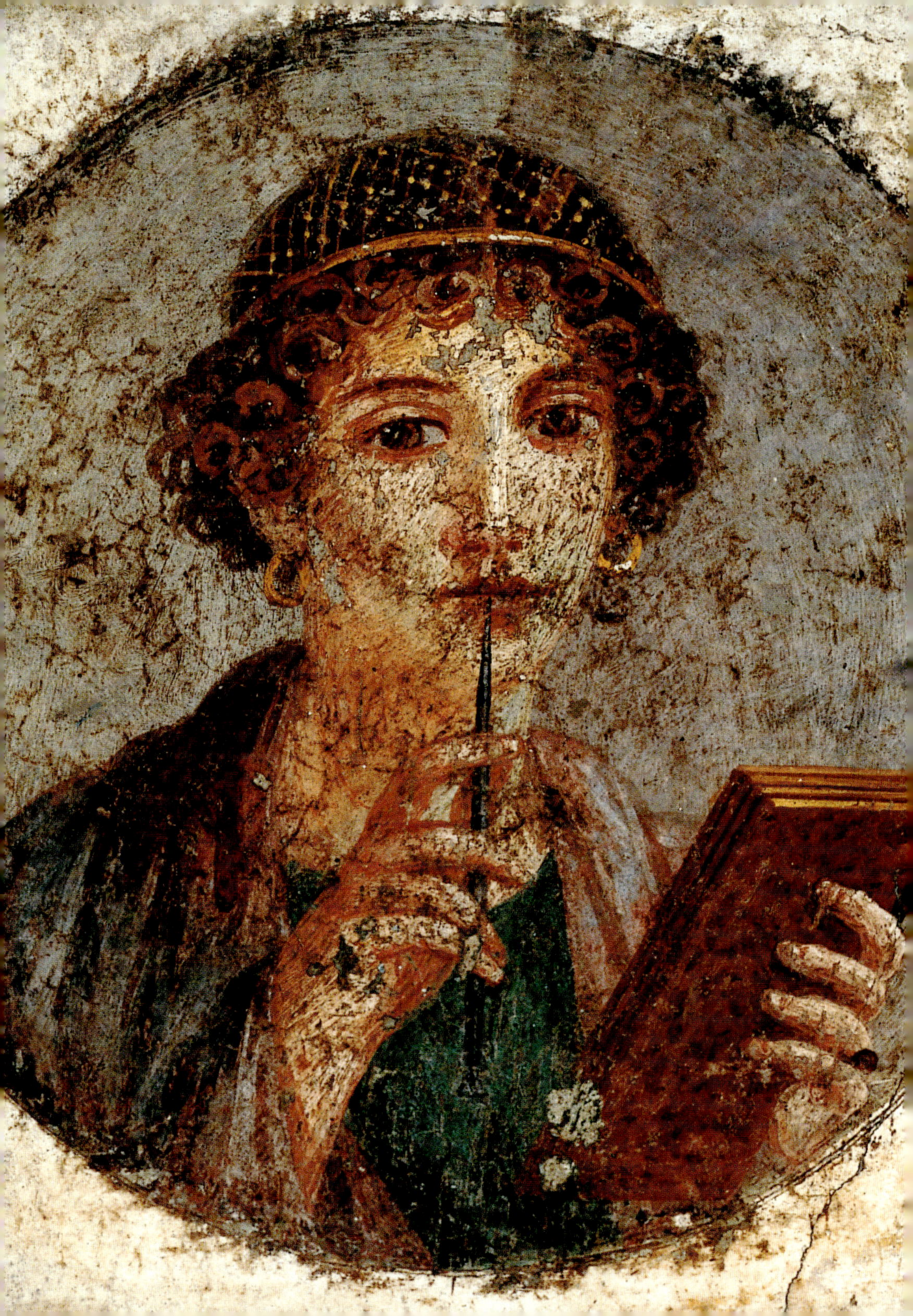

Greek Beauty

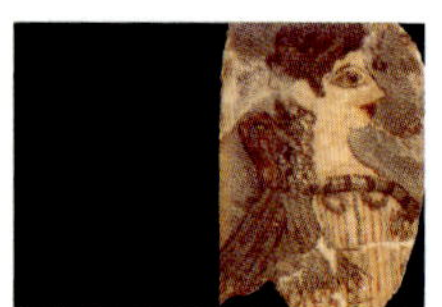

Portrait of a Woman, known as "La Parisienne," c. 1500–1450 B.C. Polychrome fresco, Knossos. Archeological Museum, Herakleion. Archeologists at the palace at Knossos were so enchanted by this anonymous coquette, with her full lips, tiny chin, and mischievous nose, that they gave her the delightful nickname of "La Parisienne." In fact, the young Minoan portrayed on this fresco was probably the priestess of some mysterious cult, as witnessed by the strange red ribbon tied behind her shoulders. © Lessing/AKG Paris.

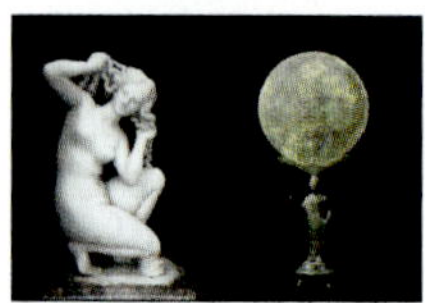

Crouching Aphrodite, 1st century B.C. Marble from the end of the Hellenistic period, school of Alexandria, Archeological Museum, Rhodes. This Aphrodite, surprised in the act of bathing, wringing seawater from her hair, is nevertheless a highly religious image. **Mirror,** handle in the form of a woman wearing a peplos, c. 460 B.C. Bronze. Kanellopoullos Museum, Athens. Much more than a mere toilet accessory, the mirror was the Greek woman's principal instrument of seduction. Even when represented in simple outline, it evoked a specifically female environment. © G. Dagli Orti, Paris.

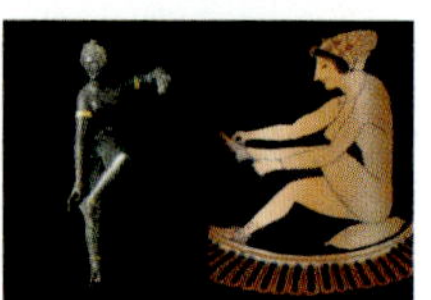

Aphrodite Unfastening her Sandal (inlaid gold jewelry). Bronze, Greco-Roman, h. 20 cm, Syria (?). Musée du Louvre, Paris. © Lewandowski/RMN. **Young Woman Fastening her Sandal,** red-figure amphora, c. 525–515 B.C. Terracotta, h. 38.5 cm. Musée du Louvre, Paris. © Lessing/AKG Paris. Like sculptors, vase painters frequently immortalized the graceful gesture of the goddess of love, or of a simple courtesan, fastening or unfastening her sandal. Whether it be on the heights of Mount Olympus or in the plush comfort of a house of pleasure, isn't femininity essentially the same?

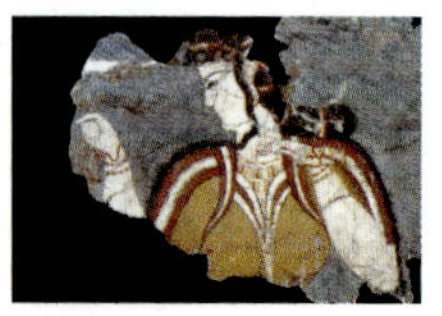

Woman, known as the "Lady of Mycenae," 13th century B.C. Fresco from a place of worship at Mycenae. National Archeological Museum, Athens. This fragment from an admirable fresco is too incomplete to be deciphered. Standing out against a strong blue background, this elegant young woman with her coiled hair (probably a goddess) has an attractively haughty bearing accentuated by her refined jewels. Despite its warlike character, the Mycaenean civilization that produced this image clearly had a liking and flair for the delights of physical beauty. © G. Dagli Orti, Paris.

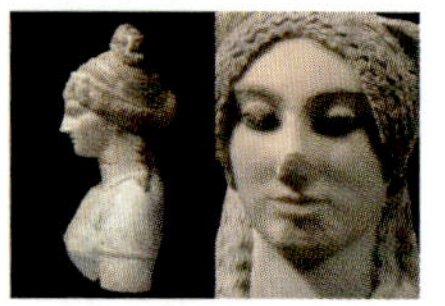

Bust of Aphrodite, 2nd century B.C. Terracotta, h. 25 cm, Myrina. Musée du Louvre, Paris. © Lewandowski/RMN. **Archaic kore,** c. 500 B.C. Marble, neo-Ionian style. Acropolis Museum, Athens. © G. Dagli Orti, Paris. These two sculptures were made nearly four centuries apart, and yet they are characterized by the same refined, sensual treatment of the braids and coils, taking the sculptural depiction of hair to new heights. One, however, is an austere Archaic ex-voto (right), while the other is an exquisite Hellenistic Aphrodite with a slightly old-fashioned charm.

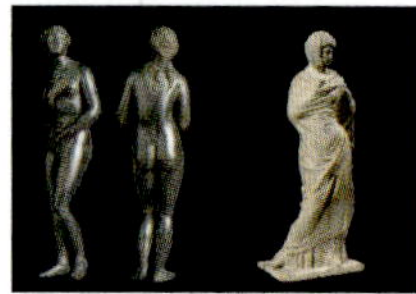

Aphrodite, 2nd century B.C. Bronze (eyes encrusted with silver), h. 24.5 cm. Sidon (Syria). Musée du Louvre, Paris. Discovered at Saida (formerly Sidon), this "Aphrodite Pudica" is thought by certain archeologists to be a more modest version of a statue created by Scopas, the great 4th-century B.C. sculptor. **"The Sophoclean"** (woman wearing a himation), c. 330 B.C. Terracotta, h. 32 cm, Tanagra. Musée du Louvre, Paris. This small terracotta statue, no doubt dressed like the women of Athens when they strolled the streets of the city, almost looks like a fashion figurine! © Lewandowski/RMN.

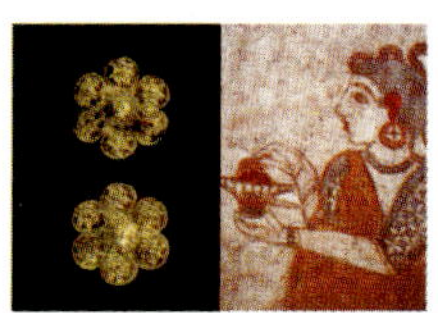

Rosettes, Mycenean art. Gold, Melos. National Archeological Museum, Athens. © G. Dagli Orti, Paris. **Woman Carrying an Incense Burner** (detail), c. 1200 B.C. Polychrome fresco, island sof Thera (Santorin), National Archeological Museum, Athens. © Dagli Orti/Corbis. Discovered on the island of Thera, this fresco probably depicts a priestess performing some sacred rite. Dressed in a long tunic, the young woman holds in her hands an incense burner and is spreading incense. On her beautiful face, which is shown in profile, can be seen a strange blue skullcap out of which a few stray locks poke—an accessory peculiar to this flourishing port city....

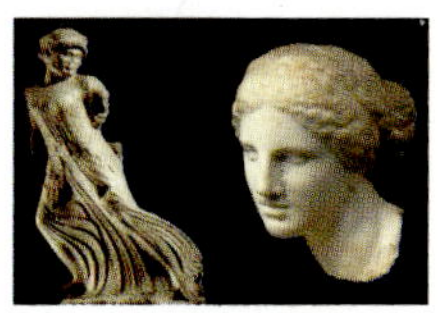

Fleeing Maenad, 5th century B.C. Stone pediment of the sacred house. Archeological Museum, Eleusis. © Lessing/AKG Paris. **Head of Aphrodite of Cnidus,** known as the "Kaufmann Head," 2nd century B.C. Marble (restored), h. 35 cm, Tralles. Musée du Louvre, Paris. © Lewandowski/RMN. On the one hand, the wild, irrational motion of a maenad in flight, the folds of her tunic swirling in the wind; on the other, impassive and regal, the face of Aphrodite reigning over the hearts and senses of mortals and gods alike. However, the goddess's liquid gaze and her full, slightly open lips almost make one forget her sacred character.

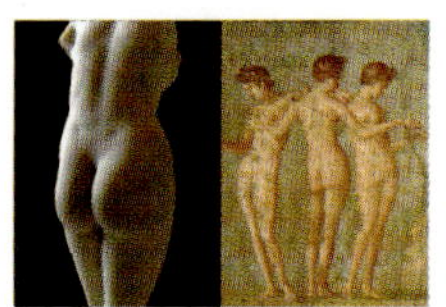

Aphrodite of Cnidus, c. 350 B.C. Marble, replica of an original by Praxiteles, h. 122 cm, Greece. Musée du Louvre, Paris. One of the most famous sculptures of Antiquity, the Aphrodite of Cnidus, if some of the spiciest anecdotes are to be believed, provoked wild erotic passion among the goddess's faithful followers. **"The Three Graces,"** 1st–3rd century. Polychrome fresco, copy of a Greek original, Pompeii. Museo Nazionale Archeologico, Naples. The copy of a Greek original that has since disappeared, this painting from Pompeii demonstrates the popularity of Greek statuary among the wealthy inhabitants of the town. © Lessing/AKG Paris.

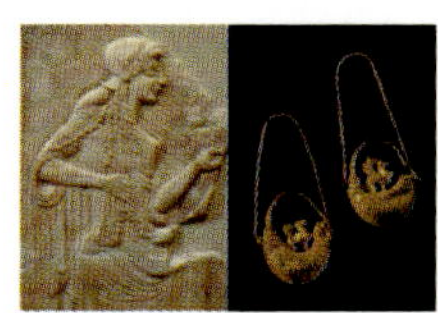

Athena Receiving Offerings, votive relief, c. 500 B.C. Archaic art, Athens. Museum of the Acropolis. **Earrings,** 4th–3rd century B.C. Gold. Museum, Volos. © G. Dagli Orti, Paris. Very different from the severe Athenas of the Classical period, this Archaic Athena seems to be the little sister of the korai discovered on the Acropolis. Of gossamer lightness, her transparent tunic reveals more than it conceals the youthful curves of her body, while here elegant locks tumble down her breasts and shoulders. Will she dare to adorn her earlobes with one of these magnificent drop earrings?

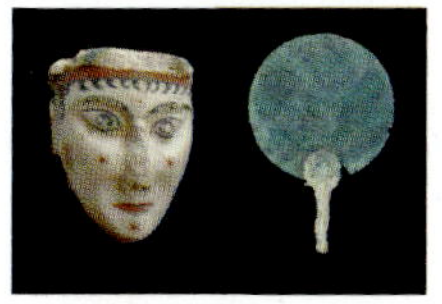

Head of a Sphinx, 14th–13th B.C. Painted plaster, Mycenae. National Archeological Museum, Athens. This hypnotic mask in painted plaster may represent a sphinx, a subject that was very popular in the Sub-Mycenaean period. The color of the face, white, indicates in conventional fashion that the monster is female, the rosettes of red dots on the cheeks, the chin, and the forehead were related to sacred tattooing practices. **Mirror,** 16th century B.C. Ivory and bronze, Mycenaean art, Pylos. National Archeological Museum, Athens. The extreme spareness of this mirror dating from the Mycenaean period is captivating. © G. Dagli Orti, Paris.

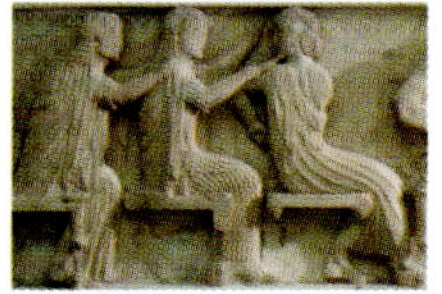

Aphrodite, Artemis, and Apollo, c. 525 B.C. Marble, h. 60 cm, east frieze of the Treasury of Siphnos. Museum, Delphi. If Herodotus is to be believed, the Treasury of Siphnos was one of the most beautiful monuments at Delphi. The inhabitants turned it into an oracular shrine to Apollo. This frieze of unprecedented finesse portrays the council of the gods commenting animatedly on an episode from the Trojan War. There is no marble whiteness here: the scene was painted, with the figures set against a sky blue background and the clothing, faces, and hair accentuated by the use of pure colors (red and green). © Lessing/AKG Paris.

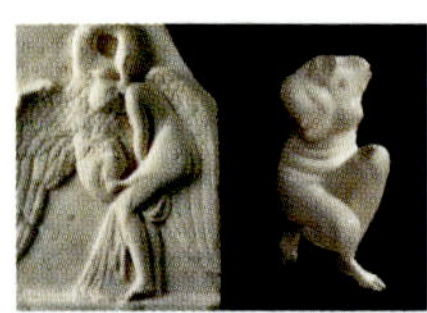

Leda and the Swan, Classical art. Marble. National Archeological Museum, Athens. In Greek mythology scenes of divine metamorphosis abound, with Zeus himself seducing a girl disguised as an animal. In this instance, he is a swan whose raised feathers frame his amorous antics. © G. Dagli Orti, Paris. **Crouching Aphrodite.** Marble, Roman replica of a Hellenistic bronze, 3rd century B.C., h. 96 cm, Musée du Louvre, Paris. No other Greek sculpture dares portray the female body in such a sensual, voluptuous manner. © Lewandowski/RMN.

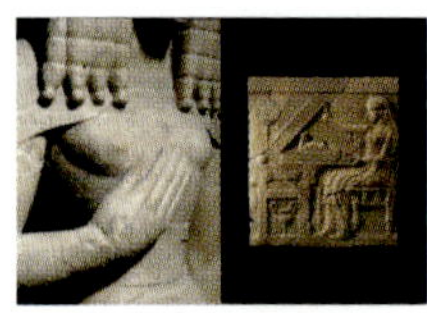

Auxerre Goddess, c. 630 B.C. Limestone, h. 75 cm, Crete (?). Musée du Louvre, Paris. © Lewandowski/AKG Paris. **Young Woman with a Casket,** votive tablet, 6th–5th century B.C. Terracotta, art of Magna Graecia, Locri. Museo Archeologico Nazionale, Reggio di Calabria. © G. Dagli Orti, Paris. On the left, the highly religious gesture of the "Auxerre Goddess" (a sculpture from the Daedalic period probably representing a dedicante, her hand placed demurely on her chest); on the right, a young woman immortalized while dressing, carefully opening her jewelry casket.

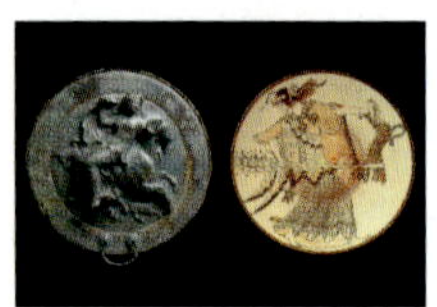

Aphrodite Pandemos ("of all the people") sitting on a goat, mirror cover, 4th century B.C. Bronze, h. 14.4 cm, necropolis of Palestrina (Praeneste). Musée du Louvre, Paris. © Lewandowski/RMN. **Maenad with snakes, a thyrsus, and a leopard,** Brygos Painter, Attic white-ground cup, c. 490 B.C. Pottery, d. 28.5 cm, from Vulci (Etruria). Staatliche Antikensammlungen, Munich. © Lessing/AKG Paris. Aphrodite in her Pandemos guise (incarnation of frivolous, vulgar, physical love) and a maenad captured in a state of ecstatic frenzy. We are a long way from the morals of the virtuous city!

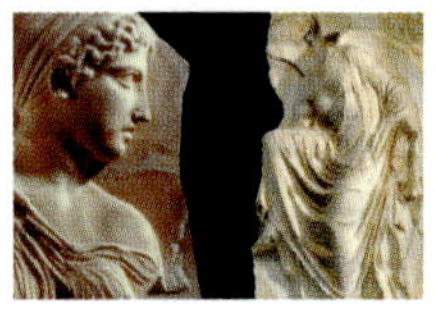

Artemis, c. 440–420 B.C. Marble from Pentelikos, workshop of Phidias, Athens, east frieze of Parthenon. Acropolis Museum, Athens. This Artemis, the incarnation of ideal beauty as conceived in the Classical period, is characterized by restrained sensuality. Her hair is held in place by a headband, while her garment barely reveals a shoulder. © Lessing/AKG Paris. **Victory Unfastening her Sandal,** c. 410–400 B.C. Limestone, Athens, sculpture from the parapet of the Temple of Athena Nike. Acropolis Museum, Athens. This Victory undoing her sandal heralds the voluptuousness of the High Classical period. © G. Dagli Orti.

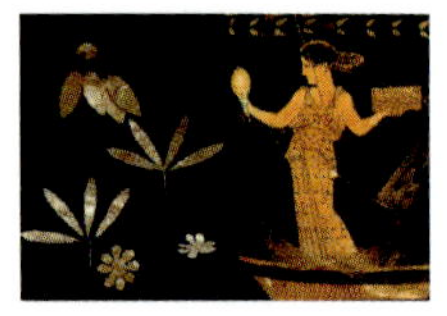

Jewelry, Early Minoan II period (c. 2500–2200 B.C.). Gold, Mochlos. Archeological Museum, Herakleion. A testament to the refinement of the Minoan civilization, these small gold elements reveal the Cretans' great love of nature. © G. Dagli Orti, Paris. **Woman Holding a Mirror** and a Cosmetics Box, red-figure pyxis, c. 420–410 B.C. Pottery, Skyphos. Musée du Louvre, Paris. Is this coquette, who has two of the emblems of beauty—a mirror and a box for cosmetics and ointments—getting ready for her husband? © Lessing/AKG Paris.

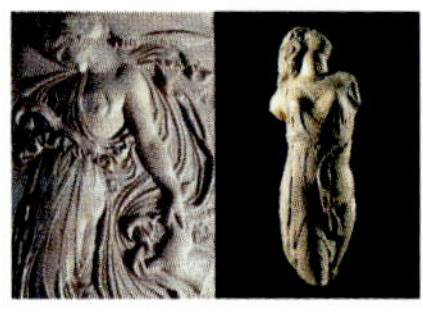

Dancing Maenad, Callumachus (after), bas-relief from a round altar, 5th century B.C. Marble, Roman copy, h. 135.5 cm. Capitoline Museum, Rome. **Maenad,** Scopas (after), c. 370–330 B.C. Marble, Roman copy of a lost Greek original, h. 45 cm, Marino (?), Staatliche Kunstsammlungen, Dresden. In sharp contrast to the sensible Athenian woman confined to the protective environment of the gynaeceum, the maenad is the quintessential outsider, the "wild woman" who follows the wanderings of Dionysus, the god of drunkeness and altered states. Sometimes she twirls in an ecstatic dance and sometimes she collapses in desperation. © Lessing/AKG Paris.

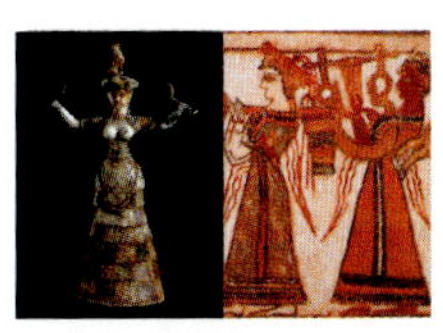

"Snake Goddess," c. 1500 B.C. Faience, Knossos. Archeological Museum, Herkaleion. Despite her diminutive size (a few centimeters high), this little statue has enormous expressive power and probably represents a chthonian divinity unique to the Cretan world. She seems to be linked to the underworld, as suggested by the two snakes that she holds in her hands. © G. Dagli Orti, Paris. **Sarcophagus of Aghia Triada** (detail), c. 1400 B.C., fresco painted on stone. These men and women carry offerings in their arms and are dressed in the Minoan manner, with long, brightly colored tunics. © Corbis.

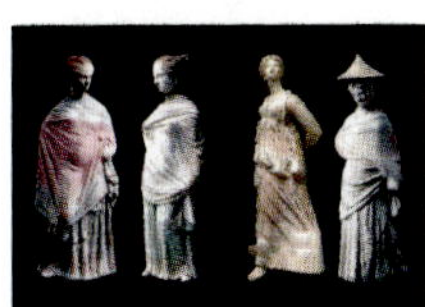

Tanagras. This is a veritable "fashion show" in miniature. From left to right: *Young woman*, 3rd century B.C., polychrome terracotta, Tanagra (Greco-Roman Museum, Alexandria). © De Luca/Corbis. *Young Woman wearing a himation*, c. 320–300 B.C., terracotta, polychrome, h. 22.5 cm, Tanagra, Musée du Louvre, Paris. © Lewandowski/RMN. *Phainomerides Victory (?)* ("with bare thighs"), c. 150–100 B.C., terracotta, h. 32 cm, necropolis of Myrina (Musée du Louvre, Paris). © Lewandowski/AKG Paris. *Young Woman with Conical Hat*, 3rd century B.C., polychrome terracotta, Tanagra (Greco-Roman Museum, Alexandria). © De Luca/Corbis.

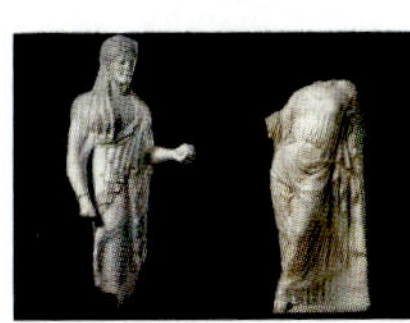

Kore from the Acropolis, c. 520–510 B.C. Marble, h. 115 cm, Acropolis, Athens. Acropolis Museum, Athens. © Nimatallah/AKG Paris. **Aphrodite with Pillar,** Alcamenes (after), c. 420–410 B.C. Marble, h. 118 cm, Greece. Musée du Louvre, Paris. © Lewandowski/RMN. A century and two radically different approaches separate this austere Archaic kore (left) and this quivering Aphrodite. These two images of beauty are also two images of the sacred: one distant and hieratic, the other all too human!

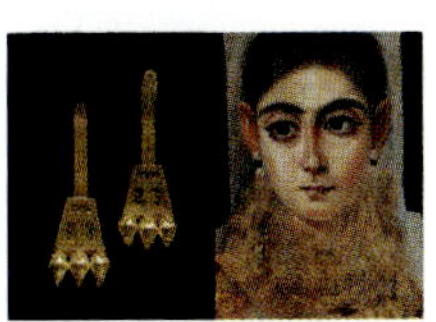

Ear pendants, 850 B.C. Gold, tomb, Athens. Museum of the Ancient Agora, Athens. © G. Dagli Orti, Paris. **Portrait of a Young Woman, known as "L'Européenne,"** from Antinopolis, c. 117–138 B.C. Encaustic painting and gold leaf on a wooden panel. Musée du Louvre, Paris. © RMN, Paris. In addition to their undeniable power, the portraits from Roman times found in the Fayum region of Egypt reveal the fondness for clothes and jewelry among these distant descendants of Alexander and Cleopatra. They are like a fragment of ancient Greece transplanted to the heart of the kingdom of Isis and Osiris.

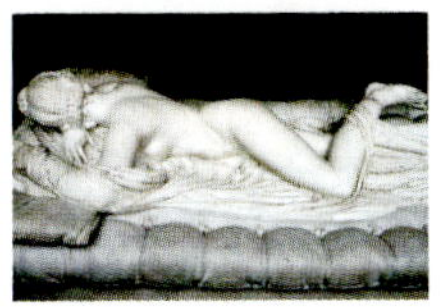

Sleeping Hermaphrodite, 6th–1st century B.C. Luni marble, replica of an original created around the 2nd century B.C., l. 148 cm, Rome. Musée du Louvre, Paris. Neither man, nor woman, but both at the same time, this ambiguous creature was popular in the Hellenistic period, which had a taste for the bizarre and, on occasion, for nefarious eroticism. Lying on a mattress executed centuries later by Bernini, this sculpture also demonstrates the sickly vapidity that tinged many replicas of the late period. In other words, this is "Praxiteles revised and updated with a Roman flavor." © Lessing/AKG Paris.

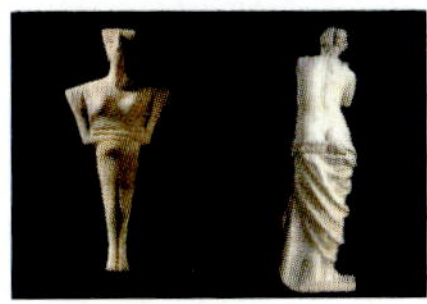

Cycladic idol, c. 2800–2300 B.C. Marble, h. 46 cm, island of Syros, National Archeological Museum, Athens. © Lessing/AKG Paris **Aphrodite, known as the "Venus de Milo,"** c. 100 B.C. Marble, h. 202 cm, Milo. Musée du Louvre, Paris. © Arnaudet/Schormans/RMN. On the one hand, the female body reduced to a simple sketch, a miracle of perfect geometry; on the other, the back whose sensuality has mesmerised generations of visitors to the Louvre. A striking summary of the history of beauty and its representation in Greek lands over more than three millennia.

At the risk of repeating herself from one book to the next, the author would like to express her heartfelt gratitude to Laurent and Cassandre Schneiter, those two lovers of ancient Greece, and also to Martine Assouline, who believed in this book, and Julie David for her kindness and constant support.